CONTENTS

Page	
1	Title Page
2	Credits
3	Contents
4-8	Fishing in Pennsylvania
9-11	Types of Artificials
12-13	Types of Baits
14-15	Selecting the Artificial
16	Pennsylvania Emergence Chart
17	Fly Fishing Only Projects
20	Delayed Harvest Fly Fishing Only
23	No Harvest Fly Fishing
24	Catch and Release
25	Delayed Harvest, Artificial Lures Only
27	Trophy Trout Projects
27	Wild Trout Waters, Limestone Streams
28	Miscellaneous Special Regulations
32-33	Palomino Trout
34-42	Eastern Region Trout Waters
43-58	Central Region Trout Waters
59-66	Western Region Trout Waters
67-79	Top 100 Plus Streams
80-81	Law Enforcement, Stockings
82-86	Upper Delaware River Trout Fishing
87-88	Angler Recognition Program
89-95	Erie County—Coho and Chinook
96-98	Steelhead Trout
99-100	How to Properly Match Your Fly Fishing Equipment
101	Understanding the Emergence Chart
102-103	Some Trout Recipes
104	Stream Notes, Misc.

A solitary angler carefully nets a native brook trout caught in one of many cold water mountain brooks.

TROUT FISHING IN PENNSYLVANIA

When outsiders, and even some residents, think of Pennsylvania, the first impression that comes to mind is the industrial image of the state and visions of coal fields, mining towns and steel mill smoke. It is expected that everything within the state is either polluted or covered with coal dust. Well, nothing could be further from the truth.

Pennsylvania ranks as one of the nation's most productive and prosperous industrial states and boasts numerous nationally ranked firms based within its confines. Even so, Pennsylvania has a great deal to offer the outdoors person. When it comes to maintaining a level of good fishing, the Keystone state takes a backseat to none, and is ranked among the leaders in quality waters and fishing available to the population. Although the fabled streams of the Catskills and many others in the Northeast and Far West are prominently mentioned in numerous outdoor magazines, such Pennsylvania streams as Yellow Breeches, Letort, Kettle Creek, to mention a few, can compete with the best when it comes to fishing water and scenic beauty.

With careful foresight, and diligent effort, the state has halted and reversed the stream pollution problem that was so prevalent during the early part of the century. With the subsequent closing of many deep mines and the initiation of a strict reclamation program for lands affected by coal stripping, Pennsylvania anglers continue to enjoy more fishing waters, of good quality, than ever before, and more streams are constantly added to the list of those having satisfactory water to sustain trout life.

The Pennsylvania Fish Commission presently releases legal size trout in every one of the Commonwealth's sixty-seven counties, thus assuring every citizen the opportunity of having trout fishing within his locale. Within the state are 936 streams totaling 5,264.3 miles of trout stocked waters. To this figure you can add 96 ponds and lakes, or 5,306.7 acres of trout inhabited water, thus you can appreciate the enormous effort extended by the commission to promote and maintain a successful trout program.

Along with the stocking and replenishing program, additional miles of streams produce a supplemental population of naturally hatched trout, mostly brook trout, which is the official fish of the state, and a native to many of the cooler mountain streams. A trout program of the size currently maintained requires a considerable amount of teamwork from the hatchery biologist to the hatchery truck drivers to the law enforcement officers. The commission does a thorough job in every phase, which is why Pennsylvania continues to attract a rising number of anglers each year, many of them from out of state. Despite the close proximity of the Catskill Mountains to New York City and Northern New Jersey, an increasing number of NJ and NY license plates are seen along Pennsylvania trout streams, and the same holds true for other parts of the state that is convenient to fishermen from Maryland, Delaware, Ohio and West Virginia.

The commission maintains twelve fish hatcheries, of which eight are devoted strictly to trout and salmon culture. The rainbow is raised in the greatest number followed by the brown, brook and palomino. Natural brook trout propagation supplements stockings in many of the smaller streams. To give you an idea of the number of trout that are released annually in the previously mentioned waters, the commission reports that in an average season more than 2,500,000 trout are released prior to the season opener in early April. To this impressive figure you can add nearly as many more that will be released during the regular in-season plantings. When the trout opener arrives in early April eager anglers can be sure of well stocked and widely dispersed trout.

Speaking about the in-season stocking program, the commission has discarded the former system of highly publicizing the time, place and date of in-season stockings. The termination of this system was due primarily to the bad publicity and public image being created by a horde of regular, weekly tank truck followers. These fishermen were making it a weekly ritual, which was occurring every day that trout stockings were announced. Under the present schedule, trout are first planted, but the stocking data is not made public until several days afterwards. Even then, the exact date and location of the releases are not mentioned, only the bodies of water.

The system is a marked improvement over the old, but the commission says they are still striving for even better results. Stockings commence in mid-April and are concluded just before Memorial Day.

From the clear sparkling waters of the Lackawaxen in the Northeastern section to the meandering, gentle riffles of Traverse Creek in the Southwest, there is plenty of trout and a delightful variety of waters and conditions to suit your fancy. The state's 936 streams are basically open to any type of fishing, although there are numerous ones designated as fly fishing or artificial only. There are also some maintained strictly on a fish-for-fun basis. There are many small lakes and ponds stocked with trout, and for the less ambitious, it can be a matter of just tossing a bobber and worm into a small pond and relaxing. Regardless of your personal preference, there is a place somewhere in Pennsylvania for you.

In addition to the trout material contained in this guide, we have included a section pertaining to the Coho and Chinook Salmon, and Steelhead Trout that are found in the Erie County area of the state. The introduction of these superb gamefish has added a new dimension in big fish angling, and we suggest that in addition to the challenge of one of many trout streams, that you try your luck in catching one of these heavy weights of Pennsylvania.

As you study this guide you will note that its purpose is to acquaint you with the streams and their locations, plus pertinent data. This guide is not intended to teach you how to fish. There are many excellent publications on the market that will describe in detailed form how to fish for various species, and if you are inexperienced, we suggest you obtain the appropriate information.

The streams listed herein are easily located by use of a common highway map, as we have listed the streams by their county location, plus reference to the nearest town or highway access. A quick scan of your map will quickly and easily direct you to the stream of your choice.

The last part of this guide contains an index of sporting goods dealers and licensed agents, that we visited. We have always found that the best way to take any fishing trip is by taking a few minutes to plan your travel time. Take particular note of any dealers in the vicinity you are planning to visit, and either give them a call, or stop. Besides being able to satisfy your needs for equipment and bait, they represent an excellent source of information regarding current, local stream information, hot spots, etc.

Whether you are a resident or not, we hope that you will make it a point to discover a little bit of Pennsylvania sometime during the trout season. When you do, we have no doubt that you will join the ranks of those trout anglers who year after year have experienced the pleasure of Pennsylvania trout fishing. Above all, please set an example of being a good sportsman, and respect both your fellow fisherman and the private property owners. Cooperation by all concerned will continue to make Pennsylvania's trout fishing as good as any in the land, and better than most. Good luck and good fishing.

DOUBLE—EYE KNOT

1. Using the end of line or leader, tie a simple overhand knot around the standing part of the line, thus forming a loop, and run the loop through the hook eye

2. Pass loop over and around the hook bend, and draw it up near the hook eye.

3. Run end of line through loop beneath the hook shank

4. Pull tight, and the knot is complete.

ARTIFICIALS FOR PENNSYLVANIA STREAMS

Generally speaking, such time proven trout flies as the Hendrickson, Cahill, Adams, etc., are universal producers on practically any trout stream in the East, including Pennsylvania streams. In this respect, the experienced fly fisherman will probably have in his possession a well-rounded assortment of flies to suit the time, location and current hatches.

However, to the less informed, we have polled many fly fishermen who successfully ply the waters of various Pennsylvania streams, asking their opinion as to the most consistent trout producers. Accordingly, we are listing those trout flies whom our experts feel are most likely to catch trout, under most conditions, on any stream listed in this guide.

 ## Dry Flies

QUILL GORDON, very effective during the early part of the season, April and May, preferred hook sizes 10-12.

ADAMS, good on all streams and will produce throughout the season. During May and June try hook sizes 12-14, and from July to the latter part of the season, try sizes 18-20.

BLACK GNAT, a good late summer and early fall selection, preferred hook sizes 18-20.

DARK CAHILL, another good selection for all streams, being most productive after June. Preferred hook sizes 12-16.

LIGHT CAHILL, can be used on all streams with good results, best effective months are May and June, preferred hook size 12-16.

HENDRICKSON (LIGHT), very good during the early part of the season, April and May, preferred hook sizes 12-16.

MARCH BROWN, an excellent early season fly, very good during April and May, preferred hook size 12-16.

CADDIS FLY (WINGED), light brown, use either the dry or wet version, effective from June until end of season, preferred hook size 12-14.

Wet Flies and Streamers

MUDDLER MINNOW (BROWN), probably the best choice of the wet flies and can be used effectively all season. Preferred hook size 8.

MUDDLER MINNOW (WHITE), another good choice that will bring results all season long, preferred hook size 8.

GREY HACKLE, a fairly good fly during April and May until about mid-June, and will produce on all streams, preferred hook sizes 12-16.

WOOLEY WORMS, dark or light, very good during the early stages of the season, until about the end of June, also effective in the fall months, preferred hook sizes 8-10.

RED WING COACHMAN, effective all during the season, and a good alternative when nothing is working. During the early part of the season try hook sizes 8-12, after July use 12-18.

ROYAL COACHMAN, similar characteristic as the Red Wing Coachman, same data applies.

BLACK-NOSED DACE, an excellent streamer that works anytime during the season. Its resemblance to a small native minnow makes it highly attractive to the trout, preferred hook sizes 8-10.

MICKEY FINN, another fine lure, which is attractive to rainbows, preferred hook size 8-10.

LITTLE BROWN TROUT or LITTLE BROOK TROUT, as the name implies, these are brightly colored imitations of small trout, and are excellent choices in early season or high waters, preferred hook size 8-10.

Nymphs

All types of Nymphs are productive in Pennsylvania streams, and if you have a favorite that has proven successful, by all means stay with it, because it will catch trout in any Pennsylvania waters. For the inexperienced, we recommend that you consult with any sporting goods dealer in the area where you plan to fish, and they will gladly tell you which are effective in their area.

Spinning

Spinning lures, particularly those of the flashing, shimmering variety catch plenty of trout in Pennsylvania streams. For best results, we suggest using smaller ones in the hook size range of 6-10. Lures containing a moderate amount of hair or feathers are fine. The average weight should range from $1/16$ to $1/32$ ounce. Spinning lures should be complemented by a light action rod and either a 2 or 4 pound test line, monofilament, high visibility. For real sport fishing, try an ultra-light combination, which provides plenty of action even when hooking an average sized fish.

In the early stages of the season, when the streams are above normal and cloudy, it may be necessary to add one or two split-shot sinkers to your line, and should be placed about eighteen inches above your lure. In clear, lower waters, the weight of the lure should be sufficient to sink to the proper depth.

As far as any special preference, there are so many available that catch trout, that space would not permit us to list them all. Sporting goods dealers usually have an abundant selection, and they will assist in pointing out those that are the best sellers, and get the most consistent results.

A WORD ABOUT BAIT FISHING

It is generally conceded that the majority of early season anglers are bait tossers, and annually more trout fall victim to the common, ordinary garden worm that most artificials, with live minnows being another popular choice. It's easy to understand why the worm is such a good trout bait, they are highly palatable to the trout, and are found just about everywhere in the country.

During the early season, when the streams are still high and cloudy from the spring runoff of melting snows, the worm is a very effective bait, especially when fished near the bottom, kept at the proper depth by a few split shot sinkers. Impaled on a size 8 or 10 hook they will generally insure plenty of strikes and some fish.

Once the streams begin to recede and attain a state of clarity, the small minnow moves into the spotlight, and replaces the worm as the best producer. Small minnows of 1½ to 2½ inches are generally fished with just a split shot or two to keep them below the surface, and should be hooked through the upper lip with a size 8 or 10 hook. Hooking through the upper lip will keep the minnow alive for an extended period, and also insure better hook penetration, since the trout will swallow the minnow head first. When fishing streams with deep pools or on ponds and lakes, we have found the best method is to use a bobber, and allow the minnow to swim freely to attract the trout.

Another early season favorite in Pennsylvania is the salmon egg. Salmon eggs come in a variety of sizes and colors, and at any given time they will all take trout, although we have found that those flavored with cheese are more productive than others. Use a size 10 salmon hook for best results. Likewise, the same hook size is best for golden meal worms, which are also good when fished in streams containing high populations of brown trout.

In spite of the presentation of natural baits, trout have an appetite for unusual foods, and Pennsylvania fishermen have found that ordinary whole kernel corn, right from the can, and soft cheese rolled into marble sized balls, are excellent baits. You need only to bait your hook with a single kernel, and the corn will stay on indefinitely. The cheese will gradually dissolve in the water, thus you might want to add a bit of cotton to help extend the usage. Although we have tried cheese in New York and New Jersey, with little or no results, our luck in Pennsylvania has been the opposite.

Both the corn kernels and cheese balls should be fished in the same manner as a worm, keeping the bait as close to the stream bottom as possible. If you are fishing a pond or lake, simply cast the bait into a likely spot, and allow it to lie on the bottom. The trout will quickly locate it, and if feeding, will waste little time and striking.

SELECTING THE ARTIFICIAL

We can safely surmise that at one time or another all trout are going to feed. All that lies between the angler catching or not catching is to correctly determine what the trout will eat and when. It is our objective to then present our selection in a natural manner to convince the trout that "that's it, and right now," but how does our elusive prey determine whether it's to be a worm, minnow, ephomennella or a subvania?? When it comes to food selection it is usually a matter of instinct and habit, although trout are not necessarily 100 percent fish of habit. Our task is to try and fool the trout into thinking our fly is the real thing.

When a particular insect hatch is beginning or is in progress, or a spinner fall is occurring, odds will favor the probability of the trout feeding selectively. The angler will have to imitate, as close as possible, the active hatch, or to quote a phrase, "match the hatch." To offer some guidance in matching any hatches on Pennsylvania streams, we are presenting a chart of anticipated hatch dates and their common description. This will aid the angler in having the appropriate fly in his possession if and when he happens to be in the right place at the right time.

Bear in mind that merely having the exact duplication of the hatch does not automatically insure your success. You must be keenly observant of the location of the hatch and feeding trout (good polarized glasses are a must), approaching in a stealthful manner in order not to disturb the trout. Place yourself in a position to make your most effective cast and be sure to use a fine leader along with the proper hook size. After presenting your artificial with all the skill and cunning you possess, hopefully the trout will reward you by singling out your fly for his meal.

TERRESTRIAL ARTIFICIALS

During mid-summer into early fall, the following terrestrial imitations are generally good producers.

ANTS, effective all summer, keep your sizes in the 18-20 class, best color is black.

BEETLES, again keep them small, 18-20, black or brown.

CRICKETS, GRASSHOPPERS, excellent during August and September, dark colors seem to work best, sizes 18-20.

TYPES OF TERRESTRIALS

ANT   BEETLE   GRASSHOPPER

INSECT EMERGENCE CHART PENNSYLVANIA TROUT STREAMS

Common Name	Scientific Name	Approximate Emergence Date
Little Black Stonefly (3)	Taeniopteryx maura	April 15
Red Quill (1)	Ephemerella subvario	April 16
Little Black Caddis (2)	Chimarra aterrima	April 17
Red Legged March Fly (5)	Bibio femoratus	May 1
Smokey Alderfly (5)	Sialis infumata	May-Sept.
Black Midge (5)	Glyptotendipes lobiferus	May 1
Light Stonefly (3)	Isoperis signata	May 8-25
Penns Creek Caddisfly (2)	Brachycentrus numerosus	May 15
Black Quill (1)	Leptophlebia cupida	May 16
Early Brown Spinner	Leptophlebia cupidus	May 16
Yellow Spider (4)	Antocha saxicola	May 16
Stonefly (3)	Neophasganophora capitata	May 16
Spotted Sedge (2)	Hydropsyche slossonae	May 20
Pale Evening Dun (1)	Ephemerella dorothea, rotunda	May 20
March Brown (1)	Stenonema vicarium	May 21
Great Red Spinner (1)	Stenonema vicarium	May 21
Green Caddis (2)	Rhyacaphila lobifera	May 21
Dark Green Drake (1)	Hexagenia recurvata	May 23
Brown Drake (1)	Hexagenia recurvata	May 24
Ginger Quinn Dun (2)	Stenonema fuscum	May 25
Pale Evening Spinner (1)	Ephemerella dorothea, rotunda	May 26
Ginger Quill Spinner (1)	Stenonema fuscum	May 26
Fish Fly (5)	Chauliodes derricornis	May 26
Green Drake (1)	Ephemera guttulata	May 28
Black Drake (1)	Ephemera guttulata	May 28
Gray Drake (1)	Ephemera guttulata	May 28
Iron Blue Dun (1)	Leptophlebia johnsoni	May 28
Grannon (5)	Brachycentrus fuliginosus	May 29
Jenny Spinner (1)	Leptophlebia johnsoni	May 29
Brown Quill (1)	Siphlonurus guebecensis	June 1
Whirling Cranefly (4)	Tipula bella	June 1
Orange Cranefly (4)	Tipula bicornis	June 1
Golden Eyed Gauze Wing (5)	Chrysopa occulata	variable
White Mayfly (1)	Stenonema rubromaculatum	June 2
White Gloved Howdy (1)	Isonychia albomanicata	June 27
Yellow Sally (3)	Isoperia spp	June 28
Golden Spinner (1)	Potomanthus distinctus	June 28
Willow or Needle Stonefly (3)	Leuctra grandis	June 28
Stonefly Nymph (3)	Acroncuria lycorias	June 28
Brown Silverhorns (2)	Athripsades wetzeli	June 29
Big Orange Sedge (2)	Neuronia postica	June 30
Yellow Drake (1)	Ephemera varia	July 1
White Caddis (2)	Leptocella, exquisita, leptocella albida leptocella spp	July 1
Deer Fly (5)	Chrysops viltatus	variable
Green Midge (5)	Chironomus modestus	July 4

Reference key — (1) Mayfly, (2) Caddisfly, (3) Stonefly, (4) Cranefly, (5) Misc.

as compiled by C.M. Wetzel

Quality waters and abundant hatches make for excellent fly fishing in Pennsylvania. Each year thousands of non-resident anglers will test their skill on waters such as this.

FLY-FISHING ONLY PROJECTS

1. Fishing may be done with artificial flies and streamers constructed of natural or synthetic materials, so long as all flies are constructed in a normal fashion on a single hook with components wound on or about the hook. Specifically prohibited are the use of molded facsimiles or replicas of insects, earthworms, fish eggs, fish or any invertebrate or vertebrate either singly or in combination with the other materials. Likewise prohibited are other lures commonly described as spinners, spoons, or plugs made of metal, plastic, wood, rubber or like substance or a combination thereof.

2. Fishing must be done with tackle limited to fly rods, fly reels and fly line with a maximum of 18 feet in leader materials or monofilament line attached. Spinning, spincast and casting rods and reels are prohibited.

3. The use or possession of any natural bait, baitfish, fishbait or the use of any other devices, natural or synthetic, capable of catching fish other than the artificial flies and streamers, is prohibited.

4. Open to fishing the year-round (no closed season).

5. Fishing Hours: One hour before sunrise to one hour after sunset (except opening day of the regular trout season which is 8 a.m.).

6. Minimum Size: Nine (9) inches, caught on or in possession on, the waters under regulation.

7. Daily Creel Limit: Three (3) trout — combined species — except during the period March 1 to the opening day of regular trout season when no trout may be killed, or had in possession on, the waters under regulation.

8. Taking of Baitfish or Fishbait is prohibited.

ADAMS: *Conewago Creek* — 1 mile; From ⅛ mile below Rt. T-340, downstream to Rt. 34.

CARBON: *Mud Run* — 2.6 miles; In Hickory Run State Park

CHESTER: *French Creek* — 1.2 miles; From the dam at Camp Sleepy Hollow downstream to Sheeder Road.

CLEARFIELD: *Trout Run* — 1.5 miles; From one mile above Rt. 879 upstream to and including the Trout Run Corp. property.

CLINTON: *Young Women's Cr.* — 5.5 miles; From State Forest property line upstream to Beechwood Trail.

CUMBERLAND: *Green Spring Creek* — 1 mile; On former C.F. Beckner property.

ELK: *Mill Creek* — 1 mile; From Nagle Bridge to headwaters of Norton Reservoir Dam.

FAYETTE: *Dunbar Creek* — 4.1 mile; From the confluence of Glade Run and Dunbar Creek downstream to the stone quarry along Rt. 26047.

FRANKLIN: *East Branch Antietam Cr.* — 1 mile; From Rt. 16 downstream to Rt. T-365.

LEHIGH: *Little Lehigh Creek* — 1 mile; From Lauderslager's Mill Dam upstream to Rt. T-508.

LYCOMING: *Slate Run* — 6.5 miles; Brown Twp. — from mouth upstream to Lycoming/Tioga County line.

LYCOMING: *Loyalsack Creek* — 3 miles; From Lycoming County Line downstream to Sandy Bottom.

LYCOMING: *Gray's Run* — 2.5 miles; From Gray's Run Hunting Club property line downstream to concrete bridge at old CCC camp.

MONROE: *Big Bushkill Cr.* — 6 miles; On the Ressica Falls Scout Reservation property except 200 yds. on each side of the falls.

POTTER: *Cross Fork Creek* — 5.4 mile; From Bear Trap Lodge downstream to the Weed property.

POTTER: *Lyman Run* — 4 miles; Lyman Run Lake upstream to Splash Dam Hollow.

SOMERSET: *Clear Shade Creek* — 1 mile; From cable at Windber Water Dam, upstream.

TIOGA: *Francis Branch Tributary to Slate Run* — 2 miles; From mouth upstream to Kramer Hollow.

TIOGA: *Slate Run* — .5 mile; From the county line upstream to confluence of Cushman & Francis Branch.

VENANGO: *Little Sandy Cr.* — 2.5 miles; From L.R. 60073 at Polk upstream to old bridge at Polk Center pump house.

WAYNE: *Butternut Creek* — 2.5 miles; From L.R. 63004 downstream to mouth.

WYOMING: *Bowman Creek* — 1 mile; From the vicinity of Rt. 292 downstream to near the confluence with Marsh Creek.

YORK: *Muddy Creek* — 2 miles; From L.R. 60064 Bridge in Bridgeton up to Bruce.

DELAYED HARVEST FLY-FISHING ONLY

1. Fishing may be done with artificial flies and streamers constructed of natural or synthetic materials, so long as all flies are constructed in a normal fashion on a single hook with components wound on or about the hook. Specifically prohibited are the use of molded facsimiles or replicas of insects, earthworms, fish eggs, fish or any invertebrate or vertebrate either singly or in combination with the other materials. Likewise prohibited are other lures commonly described as spinners, spoons, or plugs made of metal, plastic, wood, rubber or like substance or a combination thereof.

2. Fishing must be done with tackle limited to fly rods, fly reels and fly line with a maximum of 18 feet in leader materials or monofilament line attached. Spinning, spincast and casting rods and reels are prohibited.

3. The use or possession of any natural bait, baitfish or fishbait, and the use of any other device, natural or synthetic, capable of catching fish other than artificial flies and streamers is prohibited.

4. Open to fishing the year-round (no closed season).

5. Fishing Hours: One hour before sunrise (except opening day of the regular trout season which is 8 a.m.) to one hour after sunset.

6. Minimum Size: Nine (9) inches, caught on, or in possession on, the waters under regulation from June 15 to the last day of February.

7. Daily Creel Limit: Three combined species from June 15 to the last day of February, only, caught on or in possession on the waters under regulation.

8. Taking of Baitfish or Fishbait is prohibited.

Handle your catch carefully so that the trout you catch and release will live to provide another angler with a challenge.

BEDFORD: *Yellow Creek* — 1 mile; From mouth of Maple (Jacks Run) upstream to Red Bank Hill.

CAMERON: *Driftwood Branch, Sinnemahoning Creek* — 1 mile; From the Shippen Township Building downstream to near Rt. 120 west of Emporium.

DAUPHIN: *Clarks Creek* — 2 miles; PGC parking area on Rt. 325 downstream to PGC access road at the Iron Furnace.

DELAWARE: *Ridley Creek* — 1 mile; From the falls in Ridley Creek State Park, downstream to the mouth of Dismal Run.

ELK: *West Branch of Clarion River* — 0.5 mile; From intersection of Rt. 219 and L.R 24007, upstream to Texas Gulf Sulphur Property. Fishing permitted from east shore only.

INDIANA: *Little Mahoning Creek* — 4 miles; From L.R. 32089 at Rochester Mills upstream to Cesna Run.

JEFFERSON: *North Fork of Redbank Creek* — 2 miles; From Rt. 322 in Brookville upstream two miles.

LANCASTER: *Donegal Creek* — 2 miles; From 275 yards below Rt. 772 downstream to Rt. T-334.

LANCASTER: *West Branch Octararo Creek* — 1.9 miles; From about 220 yards below Rt. 472, downstream to near the second unnamed tributary below L.R. 36010.

LAWRENCE: *Slippery Rock Cr.* — 0.5 mile; From Heinz Camp property downstream to ¼ mile below L.R. 37052 Bridge.

McKEAN: *Marvin Creek* — 0.9 mile; From proximity of high voltage line (3 mi. south of Smethport) downstream 0.9 mile.

UNION: *White Deer* — 2.5 miles; From Cooper Mill Road upstream to Union/Centre county line.

WARREN: *Caldwell Creek* — 1.2 miles; From Selkirk highway bridge downstream to near the Dotyville bridge.

WAYNE: *Dyberry Creek* — 1 mile; From the Widmer property line about one mile below Tanner's Falls downstream to Mary Wilcox bridge, L.R. 63041.

NO HARVEST FLY-FISHING ONLY

1. Fishing may be done with artificial flies and streamers constructed of natural or synthetic materials, so long as all flies are constructed in a normal fashion on a single barbless hook with components wound on or about the hook. Specifically prohibited are the use of molded facsimiles or replicas of insects, earthworms, fish eggs, fish or any invertebrate or vertebrate either singly or in combination with the other materials. Likewise prohibited are other lures commonly described as spinners, spoons, or plugs made of metal, plastic, wood, rubber or like substances or a combination thereof.

2. Fishing must be done with tackle limited to fly rods, fly reels and fly line with a maximum of 18 feet in leader materials or monofilament line attached. Spinning, spincast and casting rods and reels are prohibited.

3. The use or possession of any natural bait, baitfish or fishbait and the use of barbed hooks or any other fishing device other than barbless hook, artificial flies or streamers is prohibited.

4. Fishing Hours: One hour before sunrise to one hour after sunset.

5. No trout may be killed or had in possession.

6. No closed season.

A beautiful rainbow trout, totally exhausted, and skillfully landed by the angler. In a few moments it will be released to live another day.

7. Wading is permitted unless otherwise posted.

8. Taking of baitfish or fishbait is prohibited.

CENTRE: *Spring Creek (Fisherman's Paradise)* — 1 mile; Lower boundary of Spring Creek Hatchery grounds to the upper boundary of the Paradise. (No fish may be killed or had in possession.)

LEHIGH: *Little Lehigh Creek* — 1 mile; From just above Hatchery Road downstream to near the 24th Street Bridge.

POTTER: *Kettle Creek* — 1.7 miles; From about 500 ft. below Rt. 144 upstream 1.7 miles.

CATCH-AND-RELEASE

1. Fishing may be done with artificial lures only constructed of metal, plastic, rubber, or wood or with flies or streamers constructed of natural or synthetic materials. All such lures may be used with spinning or fly fishing gear. Use of gear not described in this section is prohibited. Specifically prohibited are the use of molded facsimiles or replicas of insects, earthworms, fish eggs, fish, or any invertebrate or vertebrate either singly or in combination with the other materials. Barbed hooks are prohibited; fishing may be done with barbless hooks only.

2. The use or possession of any natural bait, baitfish or fishbait and the use of barbed hooks or any other fishing device other than barbless hook, artificial flies or streamers is prohibited.

3. Fishing Hours: One hour before sunrise to one hour after sunset.

4. No trout may be killed or had in possession.

5. Open to fishing the year-round (no closed season).

6. Wading is permitted unless otherwise posted.

7. Taking of baitfish or fishbait is prohibited.

CARBON: *Hickory Run* — 1.5 miles; From Sand Spring Run downstream to the mouth.

COLUMBIA: *Big Fishing Cr.* — 1 mile; From the confluence of the East and West Branches of Fishing Creek at Grassmere Park downstream to the lower Gary Cook property line.

CUMBERLAND: *Yellow Breeches Cr.* — 1 mile; From Boiling Spring downstream to vicinity of Allenberry.

HUNTINGDON: *Spruce Creek* — 0.5 mile; Penn State Experimental Fisheries Area (about 0.6 mile above the village of Spruce Creek).

MIFFLIN AND UNION COUNTIES: *Penns Creek* — 3.9 miles; From Swift Run downstream to R.J. Soper property line.

WARREN: *West Branch of Culdwell Creek* — 3.6 miles; West Branch bridge upstream to Three Bridge Run.

DELAYED HARVEST ARTIFICIAL LURES ONLY

1. Fishing may be done with artificial lures only constructed of metal, plastic, rubber, or wood or with flies or streamers constructed of natural or synthetic materials. All such lures may be used with spinning or fly fishing gear. Use of gear not described in this section is prohibited. Specifically prohibited are the use of molded facsimiles or replicas of insects, earthworms, fish eggs, fish, or any invertebrate or vertebrate either singly or in combination with the other materials.

2. The use or possession of any natural bait, baitfish or fishbait and the use of any other fishing device other than artificial lures, flies or streamers is prohibited.

3. Open to fishing the year-round (no closed season).

4. Fishing Hours: One hour before sunrise — except opening day which is 8 a.m. — to one hour after sunset.

5. Minimum size: Nine inches (9), caught on, or in possession on, the waters under regulation from June 15 to the last day of February.

6. Daily creel limit: Three combined species from June 15 to the last day of February, only, caught on or in possession on the waters under regulation.

7. Taking of baitfish or fishbait is prohibited.

BERKS: *Tulpehocken Cr.* — 4.1 miles; From the first deflector below Blue Marsh Dam downstream to 225 yards above the junction of T-702 and T-602.

CHESTER: *Middle Branch White Clay Cr.* — 1.7 miles; From L.R. 15019 downstream to the confluence with the East Branch.

FOREST: *East Hickory Cr.* — 1.7 miles; From Queen Creek Bridge downstream to Otter Creek Bride.

MERCER: *Cool Spring Creek* — 1.25 miles; From L.R. 43027 Bridge upstream to the abandoned railroad grade.

MONROE: *Tobyhanna Cr.* — 1 mile; From the confluence of Still Swamp Run, downstream to the PP&L service bridge.

SOMERSET: *Laurel Hill Cr.* — 2.2 miles; From Laurel Hill State Park at B.S.A. Camp downstream to Rt. T-364.

WESTMORELAND: *Loyalhanna Cr.* — 1.5 miles; From Rt. 711 downstream to L.R. 64071.

YORK: *Codorus Cr.* — 3.3 miles; From L.R. 66009 downstream to Rt. 116.

TROPHY TROUT PROJECTS

1. Fishing may be done with artificial lures only, constructed of metal, plastic, rubber or wood, or flies or streamers constructed of natural or synthetic materials. All lures may be used with spinning or fly fishing gear. Anything other than these items is prohibited. Specifically prohibited are the use of molded facsimiles or replicas of insects, earthworms, fish eggs, fish or any invertebrate or vertebrate either singly or in combination with the other materials.

2. The use or possession of natural bait, baitfish and fishbait and the use of any other device natural or synthetic, capable of catching fish other than artificial lures is prohibited.

3. Open to fishing the year round (no closed season).

4. Minimum Size: 14 inches, caught on, or in possession on, the waters under regulation.

5. The daily creel limit is two trout — combined species — except during the period March 1 to the opening day of regular trout season when no trout may be killed, or had in possession, on the waters under regulation.

6. Taking of baitfish or fishbait is prohibited.

CLINTON: *Fishing Creek* — 5 miles; From the bridge at Tylersville Fish Hatchery downstream to Fleming's Bridge at Lamar Fish Hatchery.

LYCOMING AND TIOGA: *Cedar Run* — 7.2 miles; From the confluence with Buck Run downstream to the mouth.

LIMESTONE SPRINGS WILD TROUT WATERS

The same regulations apply as found under "No Harvest Fly-Fishing Only" on page 20.

CUMBERLAND: *Big Spring Creek* — 1.1 miles; from 100 feet below the source (Big Spring) downstream to the Strohm dam.

NOTE: On this project only, two trophy trout of a length of 15 or more inches may be taken daily. Barbed hooks are permitted.

Letort Spring Run — 1.5 miles; From 300 yds. above the bridge on Twp. Rt. 481 downstream to the Reading Railroad Bridge at the southern edge of Letort Spring Park.

FRANKLIN: *Falling Spring* — 2.4 miles; From near Rt. T-544 downstream to a wire fence crossing the Robert E. Gabler Farm (near I-81).

MISCELLANEOUS WATERS SPECIAL REGULATIONS

Blair and Huntingdon Counties: *Little Juniata River* — From mouth of Bald Eagle Creek (near Tyrone) downstream to the confluence of the Little Juniata River and the Frankstown Branch, Juniata River.

No closed season on trout — Daily limit opening day of trout season to Labor Day — 8 trout; day after Labor Day to succeeding day of trout season — 3 trout. Inland Regulations apply to warmwater species.

Centre County: *Spring Creek* — From bridge at Oak Hall above Neidig Brother's Limestone Co. to the mouth.

No-kill Zone — Unlawful to kill or possess any fish. All fish caught must be immediately returned. Special regulations in effect on Fisherman's Paradise and Exhibition Area near Bellefonte.

Chester County: *Valley Creek (at Valley Forge) and tributaries including Little Valley Creek.*

No-kill Zone — Unlawful to kill or possess any fish. All fish caught must be immediately returned.

Crawford County: *Finley Creek and Linesville Creek*

Spearing prohibited during walleye run each spring during such time as these streams are so posted.

Linesville Creek — from the mouth (Pymatuning Sanctuary) upstream about ½ mile to the Conrail railroad bridge, north of Rt. 6 in Linesville.

Closed to all fishing as nursery waters from March 1 to April 1.

Huntingdon County: *Stone Valley Lake*

Trout — Standard Inland Regulations. All other species — no closed season and no possession limit.

Raystown Lake and Raystown Branch — From dam downstream to Juniata River — Trout (all species) no closed season. Creel limit 8 per day during regular season; 3 per day from the day after Labor Day till opening day of next Regular Season. Size limit, Inland Rules apply.

Lebanon County: *Marquette Lake and Indiantown Gap Run and its tributaries*

Artificial lures only. (Fishing may be done with artificial lures only, constructed of metal, plastic, rubber or wood; or flies or streamers constructed of natural or synthetic materials. All such lures may be used with spinning or fly fishing gear. Specifically prohibited are the use of molded facsimiles or replicas of insects, earthworms, fish eggs, fish, or any invertebrate or vertebrate either singly or in combination with the other materials. The use or possession while fishing of any baitfish, fishbait, or natural bait, and the use of any other device not specifically authorized in this section are prohibited.)

Luzerne County: *Harris Pond*

Fishing prohibited from one hour after sunset until one hour before sunrise. Fishing prohibited from posted shore areas. Fishing limited to artificial lures only, constructed of metal, plastic, rubber, or wood or flies or streamers constructed of natural or synthetic materials. All such lures may be fished with spinning or fly-fishing gear. It is unlawful to fish with other than artificial lures on Harris Pond. Limits: Largemouth Bass: 2 per day creel limit — 15 inch minimum size limit. Inland season for ponds applies.

Mid-July and a nice trout has been netted. Note that the angler is comfortable in the water wearing only a pair of sneakers.

All other species — Inland seasons, sizes and creel limits apply. Gasoline powered motor boats prohibited. Electric motor and hand-powered boats permitted. Ice fishing is prohibited.

Luzerne County: *Lake Took-A-While*
Catfish (combined species). Limit 6 per day.

Somerset, Fayette, Westmoreland and Allegheny Counties: *Youghiogheny River* — From Reservoir to mouth of river.
No closed season on trout. Daily limit opening day of trout season to Labor Day — 8 trout, day after Labor Day to succeeding opening day of trout season — 3 trout. Inland Regulations apply to Warmwater Species.

Warren County: *Allegheny River* — 0.75 mile below Kinzua Dam.
No closed season on trout. Daily limit — 3.

Washington County: *Little Chartiers Creek* — From Canonsburg Lake Dam approximately 0.25 mile downstream to mouth.
No fishing from 12:01 a.m., March 1 to 8 a.m., opening day of trout season.

Wayne County: *Upper Woods Pond* — Use of live fish for bait is prohibited.

Fly fishing waters offer good angling opportunities even during the cold months of the year.

PALOMINO TROUT

To the novice or angler who has never sighted one, the initial reaction to seeing one of Pennsylvania's Palomino trout is "Wow, what a big goldfish." Not so, for since 1967 the Fish Commission has been producing a specially bred hybrid, the Palomino, which actually is a rainbow trout. It retains its bright red stripe, but is totally absent of any other natural coloring. Instead, the entire body will be either a pale yellow or an off-white.

Because of their color, Palominos are subjected to intense pressure from predators and anglers, for in clear water they are easily seen. Despite their high visibility, they are not easy to catch. It seems that nature has compensated for the loss of camouflage by giving the Palomino the ability to quickly develop extra stream intelligence. We have observed them in stretches of fly fishing waters where they were the target of heavy fishing pressure, only to see them repeatedly turn away from the best presentations while other trout in the area were being taken.

The Palomino trout is easily identified when compared to his rainbow brother.

Tippet and Hook Relation

Tippet Size	Hook Size
0x	Size 2, 4, 6
1x	Size 4, 6, 8
2x	Size 6, 8, 10
3x	Size 8, 10, 12, 14
4x	Size 10, 12, 14, 16
5x	Size 12, 14, 16, 18
6x	Size 16, 18, 20
7x	Size 18, 20, 22

Recommended Fly Lines in Relation to Waters

Fly Line Size	Water Type
Lightweight, No. 4, 5	Small trout streams
Mediumweight, No. 6, 7	Medium trout streams
Heavyweight, No. 8, 9	Rivers, lakes, bass bugs
Big Game, No. 10, 11	Salmon Fishing, Salt water

What started as an experimental project by the Fish Commission has grown in angler acceptance, and each season a sprinkling of Palomino trout are released in public waters. Upon release, they will average from nine to fourteen inches and are widely distributed throughout the state. If you are a fly fisherman, use the same patterns that are successful for rainbows. As far as live bait is concerned, we have had our best results using salmon eggs in the spring, and small garden worms thereafter.

If you are wondering about the taste, the Palomino can be prepared any way you choose, because they taste exactly the same as any other trout. Fortunately many fishermen, after taking a moment to admire their beauty, will return them to the stream, thus a good number of those caught never reach the frying pan. You may do the same.

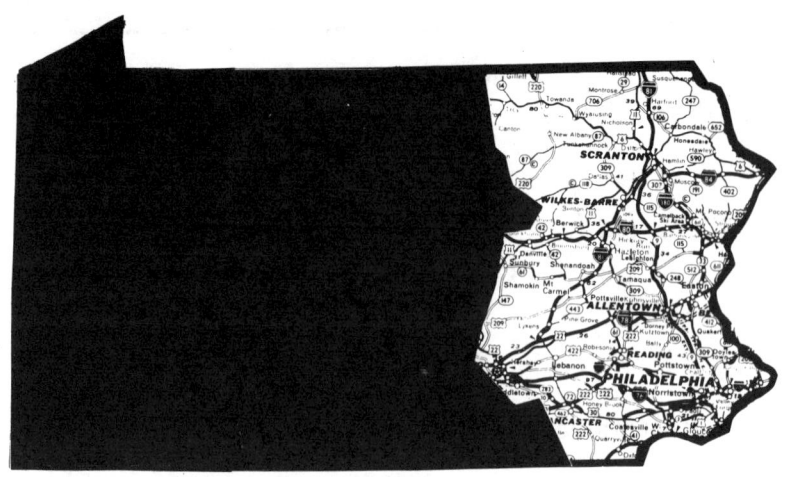

EASTERN REGION
COUNTIES

Berks, Bradford, Bucks, Carbon, Chester, Columbia, Dauphin, Delaware, Lackawanna, Lancaster, Lebanon, Lehigh, Luzerne, Monroe, Montgomery, Montour, Northampton, Northumberland, Philadelphia, Pike, Schuylkill, Sullivan, Susquehanna, Wayne, Wyoming.

NAME OF WATER	MAP REFERENCE TOWN AND HIGHWAY	SIZE
BERKS		
Allegheny Creek	Gibraltar, Rt. # 83	3.0 Miles
Angelica Creek	Shillington, Rt. # 222	3.7 Miles
Antietam Creek	Mt. Penn, Rt. # 422	2.1 Miles
Antietam Lake	Mt. Penn, Rt. # 422	15.0 Acres
Bieber Creek	Oley, Rt. # 73	7.0 Miles
Furnace Creek	Robesonia, Rt. # 422	2.5 Miles
Hay Creek	Birdsboro, Rt. # 83	7.0 Miles
Lehigh Creek, Little	Intersection, Rt. # 222 & 662	2.3 Miles
Manatawney Creek	Oley, Rt. # 73	9.0 Miles
Mill Creek Trib. to Sacony Creek	Kutztown, Rt. # 222	4.5 Miles
Schuylkill River	Hamburg, Rt. # 22	4.5 Miles
Mill Creek, Trib. to Little Swatara Creek	Bethel, Rt. # 22	2.0 Miles
Moselem Creek	Fleetwood, Rt. # 222	2.0 Miles
Northkill Creek	Shartlesville, Rt. # 22	7.5 Miles
Maiden Creek	Lenhartsville, Rt. # 78 & 22	4.3 Miles
Ontelaunee Creek	Lenhartsville, Rt. # 78	1.5 Miles
Perkiomen Creek, NW Branch	Boyertown, Rt. # 100	4.5 Miles
Pine Creek, Trib. to Maiden Creek	Lenhartsville, Rt. # 22	4.5 Miles
Sacony Creek	Kutztown, Rt. # 222	5.0 Miles
Scott's Run Lake	Birdsboro, Rt. # 83	21.0 Acres
Spring Creek	Wernersville, Rt. # 422	4.0 Miles
Swamp Creek	Morgantown, Rt. # 42	3.0 Miles
Swatara Creek	Bethel, Rt. # 501	4.8 Miles
Tulpehocken Creek	Stouchsburg, Rt. # 422	6.0 Miles
Wyomissing Creek	Shillington, Rt. # 222	2.5 Miles

NAME OF WATER	MAP REFERENCE TOWN AND HIGHWAY	SIZE
BRADFORD		
Foster Branch	Sugar Run, Rt. # 187	3.4 Miles
Millstone Creek	Powell, Rt. # 414	2.6 Miles
Mountain Lake	Burlington, Rt. # 6	34.0 Acres
Schrader Creek	Wheelerville, Rt. # 154	14.5 Miles
Schrader Creek, Little	Wheelerville, Rt. # 549	2.5 Miles
Seeley Creek	Mosherville, Rt. # 549	3.0 Miles
South Creek	Troy, Rt. # 6	9.0 Miles
Sugar Creek	East Troy, Rt. # 6	3.5 Miles
Towanda Creek	Canton, Rt. # 14	9.5 Miles
Towanda Creek, S. Br.	Stevenson, Rt. # 220	13.9 Miles
Tuscarora Creek	Silvara, Rt. # 367	6.2 Miles
BUCKS		
Delaware Canal	Newtown	15.0 Miles
Lake Luxembourg	Newtown	166.0 Acres
Levittown Lake	Levittown, Rt. # 13	20.0 Acres
Mill Creek	Doylestown, Rt. # 611	2.5 Miles
Unami Creek	Milford Square, Rt. # 663	2.0 Miles
CARBON		
Aquashicola Creek	Palmerton, Rt. # 309	5.5 Miles
Bear Creek, Big	Jim Thorpe, Rt. # 903	4.2 Miles
Buckwha Creek	Little Gap, Rt. # 904	3.0 Miles
Drakes Creek	Christmans, Rt. # 903	2.0 Miles
Fourth Run	Hickory Run State Park	4.0 Miles
Hayes Creek	White Haven, Rt. # 940	3.0 Miles
Hickory Run	White Haven, Rt. # 903	6.0 Miles
Hickory Run Dam	White Haven, Rt. # 903	3.5 Acres
Hunter Creek	Little Gap, Rt. # 309	3.0 Miles
Jeans Run	Nesquehoning, Rt. # 209	3.0 Miles
Lesley Run	Weatherly, Rt. # 193	5.0 Miles
Lizzard Creek	Bowmanstown, Rt. # 309	7.5 Miles
Mahoning Creek	Lehighton, Rt. # 209	6.0 Miles
Mauch Chunk Creek	Jim Thorpe, Rt. # 209	2.0 Miles
Mud Run	Albrightsville, Rt. # 903	2.6 Miles
Pohopoco Creek	Palmerton, Rt. # 309	4.5 Miles
Quakake Creek	Hudsondale, Rt. # 309	3.0 Miles
Sand Spring Run	White Haven, Rt. # 903	2.0 Miles
Stony Creek	Christmans, Rt. # 903	3.0 Miles
Tresckow Dam	McAdoo, Rt. # 309	1.0 Acres
CHESTER		
Beaver Run	Pughtown, Rt. # 100	3.0 Miles
Big Elk Creek	Oxford, Rt. # 1	6.9 Miles
Birch Run	Coatesville, Rt. # 30	2.0 Miles
Buck Run	Sadsburyville, Rt. # 30	4.0 Miles
Elk Creek, East Branch	Junc. U.S. Rt. # 1 & # 896	3.0 Miles
French Creek	Knauertown, Rt. # 23	14.8 Miles
Octoraro Creek, East Branch	Atglen, Rt. # 41	7.3 Miles
Pickering Crook	Chester Springs, Rt. # 113	2.1 Miles
Pocopson Creek	Pocopson, Rt. # 322	3.5 Miles
Valley Creek	Paoli, Rt. # 30	6.5 Miles
West Valley Creek	Downington, Rt. # 30	5.0 Miles
White Clay Creek	Avondale, Rt. # 1	9.5 Miles
White Clay Creek, Middle Branch	Avondale, Rt. # 1	4.6 Miles
Brandywine Creek, East Branch	Lyndell, Rt. # 282	2.5 Miles
Brandywine Creek, West Branch	Intersection # 340 and 82	2.0 Miles

NAME OF WATER	MAP REFERENCE TOWN AND HIGHWAY	SIZE
COLUMBIA		
Beaver Run	Shuman, Rt. # 44	3.0 Miles
Fishing Creek	Benton, Rt. # 254	18.5 Miles
Fishing Creek, Little	Millsville, Rt. # 422	8.0 Miles
Lick Run	Numidia, Rt. # 42	3.0 Miles
Mugser Run	Catawissa, Rt. # 42	4.6 Miles
Roaring Creek	Catawissa, Rt. # 42	14.0 Miles
Scotch Run	Mifflin Cross Roads	5.0 Miles
West Creek	Benton, Rt. # 254	4.4 Miles
DAUPHIN		
Armstrong Creek	Halifax, Rt. # 225	7.2 Miles
Clarks Creek	Dauphin, Rt. # 22	20.8 Miles
Manada Creek	Fort Hunter, Rt. # 22	4.0 Miles
Pine Creek	Klingerstown	3.9 Miles
Powells Creek	Powells Valley, Rt. # 225	11.0 Miles
Powells Creek, North Fork	Powells Valley, Rt. # 225	4.0 Miles
Powells Creek, South Fork	Powells Valley, Rt. # 225	1.7 Miles
Rattling Creek	Lykens, Rt. # 209	2.0 Miles
Rattling Creek, East Branch	Lykens, Rt. # 209	2.5 Miles
Rattling Creek West Branch	Lykens, Rt. # 209	2.5 Miles
Stony Creek	Dauphin, Rt. # 22	16.0 Miles
Wiconisco Creek	Lykens, Rt. # 209	6.7 Miles
DELAWARE		
Chester Creek	Media, Rt. # 1	3.6 Miles
Chester Creek, West Branch	Concordville	1.6 Miles
Darby Creek	Newtown Square, Rt. # 252	3.8 Miles
Ithan Run	Newtown Square, Rt. # 3	2.5 Miles
Ridley Creek	Media, Rt. # 1	8.5 Miles

Although many mountain streams do not receive hatchery trout, their natural reproduction makes them worthy of your attention.

NAME OF WATER	MAP REFERENCE TOWN AND HIGHWAY	SIZE
LACKAWANNA		
Ash Creek	Route #611	2.0 Miles
Chapman Lake	Montdale, Rt. #147	98.0 Acres
Finch Hill Park Lake	Carbondale, Rt. #6	30.0 Acres
Gardners Creek	Milwaukee, Rt. #134	5.5 Miles
Lackawanna River	Carbondale, Rt. #6	5.5 Miles
Lehigh River	Gouldsboro, Rt. #611	9.0 Miles
Rattlesnake Creek	Route #690	2.5 Miles
Roaring Brook	Elmhurst, Rt. #611	10.0 Miles
Tunkhannoch Creek, South Branch	LaPlume, Rt. #6	5.0 Miles
LANCASTER		
Bowery Run	Quarryville, Rt. #222	2.0 Miles
Beaver Creek	New Providence, Rt. #222	4.7 Miles
Chickies Creek, Lt.	Manheim, Rt. #72	3.0 Miles
Climbers Run	Martic Forge, Rt. #124	1.5 Miles
Conestoga Creek, Little	Landisville, Rt. #230	4.5 Miles
Conestoga Creek, Lt. W. Br.	Millersville	2.0 Miles
Conowingo Creek	Wakefield, Rt. #222	6.5 Miles
Donegal Creek	Marietta, Rt. #141	2.0 Miles
Donegal Springs Branch	Marietta, Rt. #141	2.0 Miles
Fishing Creek	Chestnut Level, Rt. #72	6.8 Miles
Hammer Creek	Lititz, Rt. #501	6.0 Miles
Indian Run	Ephrata, Rt. #322	2.0 Miles
Londonland Run	Paradise, Rt. #30	2.0 Miles
Middle Creek	Lititz, Rt. #501	3.5 Miles
Octoraro Creek, West Branch	Quarryville, Rt. #222	9.9 Miles
Pequea Creek	Honey Brook, Rt. #322	4.5 Miles
Rock Run	Blue Ball, Rt. #322	2.0 Miles
Seglock Run	Lititz, Rt. #501	2.0 Miles
Shearers Creek	Manheim, Rt. #72	2.5 Miles
Stewarts Run	Quarryville, Rt. #472	2.5 Miles
Swarr Run	Landisville, Rt. #230	2.0 Miles
Tuoquan Creek	Erbs Mills, Rt. #324	2.5 Miles
Muddy Creek, Little	Adamstown, Rt. #222	2.0 Miles
Cocalico Creek, Little	Reinholds, Rt. #897	2.0 Miles
LEBANON		
Bachman Run	Annville, Rt. #422	3.5 Miles
Conewago Creek	Lawn, Rt. #241	4.0 Miles
Hammer Creek	Schaefferstown, Rt. #501	2.5 Miles
Indiantown Gap Creek	Indiantown Gap, Rt. #22	1.8 Miles
Marquette Lake	Indiantown Gap, Rt. #22	14.8 Acres
Mill Creek	Newmanstown, Rt. #419	3.0 Miles
Rexmont Dam, Lower	Cornwall, Rt. #419	8.3 Acres
Rexmont Dam, Upper	Cornwall, Rt. #419	7.9 Acres
Shuey Lake	Indiantown Gap, Rt. #22	2.0 Acres
Snitz Creek	Cleona, Rt. #72	4.0 Miles
Stony Creek	Dauphin, Rt. #22	3.5 Miles
Stovers Dam	Lebanon, Rt. #422	27.0 Acres
Trout Run	Lickdale, Rt. #72	3.5 Miles
Tulpehocken Creek	Myerstown, Rt. #422	4.0 Miles

NAME OF WATER	MAP REFERENCE TOWN AND HIGHWAY	SIZE
LEHIGH		
Big Trout Run	Slatington, Rt. # 309	6.5 Miles
Cedar Creek	Allentown, W. Intersection on Rt. # 22	2.5 Miles
Coplay Creek	Coplay, Rt. # 329	5.5 Miles
Jordan Creek	Jordan Park, Rt. # 145	12.6 Miles
Lehigh River, Little	Trexlertown, Rt. # 222	14.6 Miles
Ontelaunee Creek	Kempton, Rt. # 143	7.0 Miles
Saucon Creek South Branch	Coopersburg, Rt. # 309	1.5 Miles
Swabia Creek	Macungie, Rt. # 100	3.2 Miles
LUZERNE		
Francis E. Walter Reservoir	White Haven, Rt. # 940	90.0 Acres
Bowman Creek	Noxen, Rt. # 29	6.4 Miles
Harvey Creek	West Nanticoke, Rt. # 11	13.4 Miles
Harveys Lake	Alderson, Rt. # 118	658.0 Acres
Hunlocks Creek	Hunlocks Creek, Rt. # 11	3.0 Miles
Hunlocks Creek West Branch	Hunlocks Creek, Rt. # 11	2.0 Miles
Huntington Creek	Harveyville, Rt. # 935	2.3 Miles
Irena Lake	Hazleton, Rt. # 309	20.0 Acres
Kitchen Creek	Harveyville, Rt. # 935	3.0 Miles
Lehigh River	Stoddartsville, Rt. # 115	16.3 Miles
Lehigh River (Tailwaters of Francis E. Walter Dam)	White Haven, Rt. # 940	25.0 Acres
Nescopeck Creek	Edgewood, Rt. # 309	10.0 Miles
Pine Creek	Red Rock, Rt. # 118	9.8 Miles
Sutton (Coray) Creek	Kunkle, Rt. # 309	4.0 Miles
Wapwallopen Creek	Wapwallopen, Rt. # 29	3.8 Miles
Wapwallopen Creek, Little	Wapwallopen, Rt. # 29	3.0 Miles
Wrights Creek	White Haven, Rt. # 940	6.2 Miles
MONROE		
Appenzell Creek	Stroudsburg, Rt. # 611	5.0 Miles
Aquashicola Creek	Saylorsburg, Rt. # 115	10.0 Miles
Brodhead Creek	Stroudsburg, Rt. # 611	9.0 Miles
Buckwha Creek	Kunkletown, Rt. # 904	6.1 Miles
Bushkill Creek, Big	Ressica, Rt. # 402	12.0 Miles
Dotter Creek	Kresgeville, Rt. # 209	5.5 Miles
Lake Creek	Saylorsburg, Rt. #115	3.8 Miles
McMichaels Creek	Stroudsburg, Rt. # 611	3.0 Miles
Middle Creek	Kresgeville, Rt. # 209	4.9 Miles
Pocono Creek	Stroudsburg, Rt. # 611	6.5 Miles
Pohopoco Creek	Kresgeville, Rt. # 209	12.0 Miles
Princess Run	Kunkletown, Rt. # 904	3.7 Miles
Snow Hill Dam	Canadensis, Rt. # 290	4.0 Acres
Tobyhanna Creek	Tobyhanna, Rt. # 611	6.6 Miles
MONTGOMERY		
Loch Alsh Reservoir	Ambler, Rt. # 309	7.0 Acres
Mill Creek	Bryn Mawr, Rt. # 23	2.5 Miles
Perkiomen Creek	Green Lane, Rt. # 29	3.0 Miles
Skippack Creek	Collegeville, Rt. # 422	9.0 Miles
Unami Creek	Green Lane, Rt. # 29	3.0 Miles
Wissahickon Creek	Whitemarsh	3.0 Miles

NAME OF WATER	MAP REFERENCE TOWN AND HIGHWAY	SIZE
MONTOUR		
Kase Branch	Danville, Rts. # 11 & 54	2.0 Miles
Mahoning Creek,	Danville, Rts. # 11 & 54	3.0 Miles
Mauses Creek	Danville, Rt. # 11 & 54	2.4 Miles
NORTHAMPTON		
Bertsch Creek	Walnutport, Rt. # 145	2.7 Miles
Bushkill Creek	Easton, Rt. # 22	16.0 Miles
Bushkill Creek, Little	Pen Argyl, Rt. # 702	4.5 Miles
Catasauqua Creek	Northampton, Rt. # 22	4.0 Miles
Hokendauqua Creek	Northampton, Rt. # 145	12.5 Miles
Indian Creek	Danielsville, Rt. # 93	5.0 Miles
Jacoby Creek	Portland, Rt. # 611	2.0 Miles
Martins Creek	Bangor, Rt. # 702	3.9 Miles
Martins Creek, Little	Martins Creek, Rt. # 611	2.2 Miles
Monocacy Creek	Bethlehem, Rt. # 22	11.0 Miles
Nancy Run	Butztown, Off Rt. # 22	2.8 Miles
Saucon Creek	Hellertown, Rt. # 412	5.5 Miles
Waltz Creek	Ackermanville, Rt. # 191	2.4 Miles
NORTHUMBERLAND		
Mahantango Creek	Pillow, Rt. # 225	10.5 Miles
Roaring Creek, South Branch	Elysburg, Rt. # 54	6.0 Miles
Shamokin Creek, Little	Sunbury, Rt. # 147	10.5 Miles
Zerbe Twp. Rod & Gun Club Pond	Trevorton, Rt. # 225	3.0 Acres
PHILADELPHIA		
Wissahickon Creek	Philadelphia, Rt. # 422	5.0 Miles
PIKE		
Bushkill Creek, Little	Bushkill, Rt. # 6	4.6 Miles
Decker Brook	Hawley, Rt. # 6	2.5 Miles
Fairview Lake	Tafton, Rts. # 6 & 507	195.0 Acres
Kellam Creek or Mill Brook	Hawley, Rts. # 6 & 507	2.5 Miles
Lackawaxen River	Hawley, Rt. # 6	16.0 Miles
Middle Branch Creek	Porters Lake	2.5 Miles
Saw Creek	Bushkill, Rt. # 209	5.2 Miles
Saw Kill Creek	Milford, Rts. # 6 & 507	1.5 Miles
Shohola Creek	Shohola, Rt. # 37	5.8 Miles
SCHUYLKILL		
Mahoning Creek	Schuylkill and Carbon County Line	1.0 Miles
Bear Creek	Auburn, Rt. # 895	8.5 Miles
Beaver Creek	McKeansburg, Rt. # 895	3.0 Miles
Catawissa Creek, Little	Ringtown, Rt. # 142	4.5 Miles
Deep Creek	Hegins, Rt. # 125	9.0 Miles
Lizzard Creek	Andreas, Rt. # 895	5.0 Miles
Locust Creek	Barnesville, Rt. # 45	4.7 Miles
Mahantango Creek	Klingerstown, Leg. Rt. # 53047	6.0 Miles
Pine Creek, Trib. to Mahantango Creek	Valley View, Rt. # 25	7.4 Miles
Pine Creek, Trib. to Schuylkill River	Schuylkill Haven, Rt. # 122	3.5 Miles
Pine Creek, Trib. to Schuylkill River, Little	Barnesville, Rt. # 45	2.5 Miles
Pumping Station Dam	Shenandoah, Rt. # 45	9.0 Acres

NAME OF WATER	MAP REFERENCE TOWN AND HIGHWAY	SIZE
SCHUYLKILL CO. (con't.)		
Rabbit Run Reservoir	Tamaqua, Rt. # 209	5.0 Acres
Rattling Run	Port Clifton, Rt. # 122	2.0 Miles
Swatara Creek, Lower, Little	Pine Grove, Rt. # 443	4.0 Miles
Swatara Creek, Upper	Friedensburg, Rt. # 443	6.0 Miles
Whipoorwill Dam	Frackville, Rt. # 61	6.0 Acres
Locust Lake	Barnesville, Rt. # 54	52.0 Acres
Mahanoy Creek, Little	Frackville, Rt. # 61	2.0 Miles
Neifert Creek Flood Control Reservoir	Tamaqua, Rt. # 209	6.0 Acres
SULLIVAN		
Black Creek	Cherry Mills, Rt. # 87	3.3 Miles
Double Run	Eagles Mere, Rt. # 42	2.0 Miles
Elk Creek	Hillsgrove, Rt. # 87	6.0 Miles
Fishing Creek, East Branch	Benton, Rt. # 254	5.0 Miles
Fishing Creek, West Branch	Benton, Rt. # 254	6.0 Miles
Hogland Branch	Hillsgrove, Rt. # 87	4.0 Miles
Hunters Lake	Eagles Mere, Rt. # 42	90.0 Acres
Kings Creek	Forksville, Rts. # 154 & 76	4.5 Miles
Lick Creek	Forksville, Rts. # 154 & 76	5.0 Miles
Loyalsock Creek	Forksville, Rts. # 154 & 76	20.0 Miles
Loyalsock Creek, Little	Forksville, Rt. # 87	10.0 Miles
Mehoopany Creek North Fork	Dushore, Rt. # 220	3.9 Miles
Mill Creek	Hillsgrove, Rt. # 87	3.3 Miles
Muncy Creek	Nordmont, Rt. # 154	12.0 Miles
Pole Bridge Run	Laporte, Rt. # 220	2.5 Miles
Rock Run	Muncy, Rt. # 220	5.0 Miles

Opening day in Pennsylvania has been a ritual of spring for decades. The opener attracts a large number of anglers, but there is always enough trout for all.

NAME OF WATER	MAP REFERENCE TOWN AND HIGHWAY	SIZE
SUSQUEHANNA		
Canawacta Creek, South Branch	Lanesboro, Rt. # 171 & Rt. # 92	2.5 Miles
Fall Brook	Montrose, Rt. # 106	3.5 Miles
Gaylord Creek	Rushville, Rt. # 106	7.5 Miles
Gibson Creek	Gibson, Rt. # 547	2.0 Miles
Harmony Creek	New Milford, Rt. # 11	5.0 Miles
Lackawanna Creek	Uniondale Rt. # 70	5.0 Miles
Lackawanna River	Stillwater, Rt. # 70	2.0 Miles
Meshoppen Creek	Avery, Rt. # 29	6.5 Miles
Meshoppen Creek, West Branch	Springville, Rt. # 29	5.5 Miles
Nine Partners Creek	Lenox, Rt. # 106	5.6 Miles
Quaker Lake	Brackney, off Rt. # 167	127.0 Acres
Silver Creek	Montrose, Rt. # 106	5.0 Miles
Snake Creek	Montrose, Rt. # 106	10.0 Miles
Starrucca Creek	Lanesboro, Rt. # 70	13.0 Miles
Tingley Lake	Harford, Rt. # 547	42.0 Acres
Tunkhannock Creek	Gelatt, Rt. # 92	7.0 Miles
Tunkhannock Creek, East Branch	Lennoxville, Rt. # 92	12.1 Miles
Wyalusing Creek	Montrose, Rt. # 100	2.5 Miles
Wyalusing Creek, Middle Branch	Lawton, Rt. # 106	7.0 Miles
Wyalusing Creek, North Branch	Rushville, Rt. # 106	7.0 Miles
Lackawanna Creek, East Branch	Herrick Center	2.0 Miles
Martin's Creek	Nicholson, Rt. # 92	4.7 Miles
WAYNE		
Alder Marsh Brook	Pleasant Mount., Rt. # 371	2.2 Miles
Butternut Creek	Hamlin, Rt. # 191	2.2 Miles
Duck Harbor Pond	Lookout, Rt. # 191	121.0 Acres
Dyberry Creek	Honesdale, Rt. # 6	5.8 Miles
Dyberry Creek, East Branch	Honesdale, Rt. # 6	6.0 Miles
Dyberry Creek, Middle Branch	Pleasant Mount, Rt. # 371	1.1 Miles
Dyberry Creek West Branch	Honesdale, Rt. # 6	8.5 Miles
Equinunk Creek	Poyntelle, Rts. # 170 & 370	12.0 Miles
Equinunk Creek, Little	Lookout, Rt. # 90	3.1 Miles
Holbert (Root's) Creek	East Honesdale, Rt. # 6	3.6 Miles
Hollister Creek	Hilltown (Lookout, Rt. # 90)	3.3 Miles
Lackawanna River	Pleasant Mount Hatchery, Rt. # 371	2.0 Miles
Lackawaxen River	Prompton, Rt. # 170	15.9 Miles
Lackawaxen River, West Branch	Prompton, Rts. # 6 & 170	6.8 Miles
Lake Lorain	Orson, Rts. # 370 & 670	48.0 Acres
Lehigh River	Gouldsboro, Rt. # 507	3.0 Miles
Long Pond	Aldenville, Rt. # 170	81.0 Acres
Shadigee Creek	Shehawken Corner, Rt. # 670	3.0 Miles
Shehawken Creek	Preston Park, Rt. # 247	8.4 Miles
Sherman Creek	Preston Park, Rt. # 370	2.7 Miles
Upper Woods Pond	Pleasant Mount, Rt. # 670	80.0 Acres
Van Auken Creek	Prompton, Rts. # 6 & 170	3.3 Miles
Wallenpaupack Creek	Newfoundland, Rts. # 507 & 191	8.0 Miles
Wallenpaupack Creek West Branch	Hamlin, Rt. # 90	6.0 Miles

NAME OF WATER	MAP REFERENCE TOWN AND HIGHWAY	SIZE
WYOMING		
Bowman's Creek	Noxen, Rt. # 29	18.0 Miles
Carey Lake	Tunkhannock, Rt. # 29	262.0 Acres
Horton Creek	Nicholson, Rt. # 11	3.0 Miles
Lake Winola	Lake Winola Rt. # 6	198.0 Acres
Mehoopany Creek	Forkston, Rt. # 87	9.9 Miles
Mehoopany Creek, North Branch	Forkston, Rt. # 87	6.5 Miles
Meshoppen Creek	Meshoppen Rt. # 309	8.5 Miles
Meshoppen Creek West Branch	Meshoppen, Rt. # 6	2.5 Miles
Oxbow Lake	Tunkhannock, Rt. # 6	60.0 Acres
Tunkhannock Creek, South Branch	Factoryville, Rt. # 11	6.0 Miles

IMPROVED CLINCH KNOT

Use to tie flies, bass bugs, lures, and bait hooks to line or leader. This knot reduces line strength only slightly.

1. Run the end of the line through the eye of the lure, fly, or hook, and then make at least five turns around the standing part of the line. Run the end through the opening between the eye and the beginning of the twists, and then run it through the large loop formed by the previous step.

2. Pull slowly on the standing part of the line, being careful that the end doesn't slip back through the large loop and that the knot snugs right up against the eye, and clip off the end.

FLY LINE — LEADER AND HOOK RELATION

Fly Line Size	Leader Size	Maximum Hook Size
No. 3	8x *7x 6x **5x	No. 16
No. 4	7x * 6x 5x **4x	No. 12
No. 5	6x *5x 4x **3x	No. 10
No. 6	5x *4x 3x **2x	No. 8
No. 7	4x *3x 2x **1x	No. 6
No. 8	3x *2x 1x **0x	No. 4
No. 9	2x *1x 0x **8/5	No. 2

*Most commonly used
**Not recommended sizes

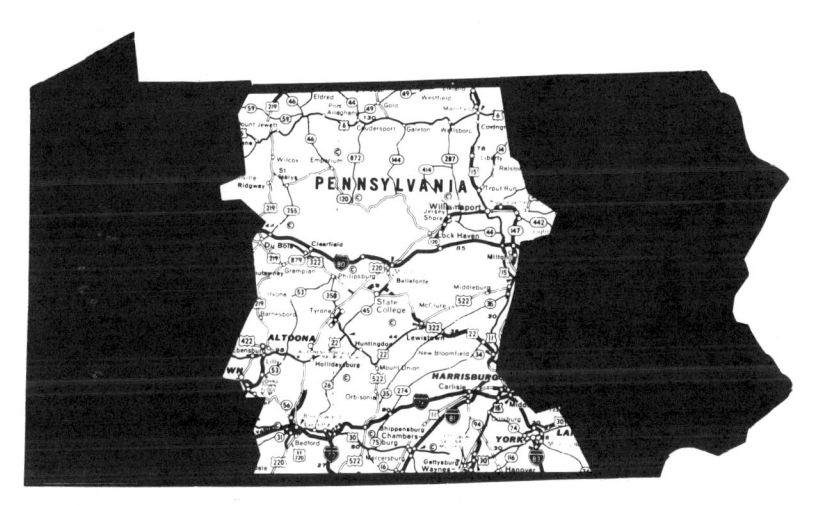

CENTRAL REGION
COUNTIES

Adams, Bedford, Blair, Cambria, Cameron, Centre, Clearfield, Clinton, Cumberland, Elk, Franklin, Fulton, Huntingdon, Juniata, Lycoming, McKean, Mifflin, Perry, Potter, Snyder, Tioga, Union, York.

NAME OF WATER	MAP REFERENCE TOWN AND HIGHWAY	SIZE
ADAMS		
Antietam Creek		
East Branch	Mont Alto. Rt. #997	1.5 Miles
Carbaugh Run	Caledonia State Park, Rt. # 30	2.5 Miles
Conewago Creek	Arendtsville, Rt. # 234	7.5 Miles
Conococheague Creek	Caledonia State Park, Rt. # 30	1.0 Miles
Latimore Creek	York Springs, Rt. # 15	4.0 Miles
Marsh Creek	Cashtown, Rt. # 01077	4.0 Miles
Marsh Creek, Little	Orrtanna, Rt. # 234	6.5 Miles
Middle Creek	Fairfield, Rt. # 116	7.0 Miles
Opossum Creek	Bendersville, Off Rt. # 34	6.0 Miles
Toms Creek	Fairfield, Rt. # 116	7.0 Miles
Waynesboro Water		
Company Reservoir	South Mountain, Rt. # 233	23.0 Acres
BEDFORD		
Beaver Creek	Loysburg, Rt. # 36	4.5 Miles
Beaverdam Creek	Queens, Rt. # 869	3.5 Miles
Beaver Run Rod & Gun		
Club Pond	Queens, Rt. # 869	1.5 Acres
Bobs Creek	Pavia, Rt. # 869	13.5 Miles
Clear Creek	Everett, Rt. # 30	7.0 Miles
Cove Creek	Charlesville, Rt. # 326	13.5 Miles
Evitts Creek	Centerville, Rt. # 220	6.5 Miles
Flintstone Creek	Md. State Line, Rt. # 40	6.5 Miles
Gladdens Run	Hyndman, Rt. # 96	4.0 Miles
Imlertown Run	Imlerton, Rt. # 30	2.5 Miles
Juniata River, Raystown		
Branch	Bedford, Rt. # 220	21.0 Miles

NAME OF WATER	MAP REFERENCE TOWN AND HIGHWAY	SIZE
Koon Lake	Centerville, Rt. # 220	268.0 Acres
Maple Run	Loysburg, Rt. # 26	2.0 Miles
Potter Creek	Waterside, Rt. # 36	3.5 Miles
Sherman Valley Run	Hopewell, Rt. # 915	6.4 Miles
Shobers Run	Bedford, Rt. # 220	5.0 Miles
Three Springs Creek	New Enterprise, Rt. # 896	2.0 Miles
Town Creek	Chaneysville, Rt. # 326	6.0 Miles
Wills Creek	Hyndman, Rt. # 96	4.0 Miles
Wills Creek, Little	Hyndman, Rt. # 96	4.5 Miles
Yellow Creek	Loysburg, Rt. # 36	14.0 Miles

BLAIR

NAME OF WATER	MAP REFERENCE TOWN AND HIGHWAY	SIZE
Bald Eagle Creek	Tyrone, Rt. # 220	5.3 Miles
Beaverdam Creek	Sproul, Rt. # 220	2.1 Miles
Bells Gap Run	Bellwood, Rt. # 865	3.8 Miles
Big Fill Run	Bald Eagle, Rt. # 220	2.0 Miles
Blair Gap Run	Duncansville, Rt. # 22	5.5 Miles
Bobs Creek	Blueknob, Rt. # 164	3.5 Miles
Camp Anderson Pond	Camp Anderson, off Rt. # 220	.8 Acres
Canoe Creek	Canoe Creek Rt. # 22	7.5 Miles
Canoe Lake	Canoe Creek, Rt. # 22	123.0 Acres
Clover Creek	Williamsburg, Rt. # 866	17.5 Miles
Juniata River, Frankstown Branch	Claysburg, Rt. # 220	6.5 Miles
Piney Creek	Williamsburg, Rt. # 866	6.0 Miles
Poplar Run	Newry, Rt. # 220	7.0 Miles
Riggles Gap Run	Pinecroft, Rt. # 220	2.0 Miles
Smokey Run Rod & Gun Club Pond	Claysburg, Rt. # 220	1.0 Acres
South Poplar Run	Claysburg, Rt. # 220	4.0 Miles
Tipton Run	Tipton, Rt. # 220	4.5 Miles
Vanscoyoc Run	Bald Eagle, Rt. # 220	3.5 Miles

CAMBRIA

NAME OF WATER	MAP REFERENCE TOWN AND HIGHWAY	SIZE
Beaver Dam Run. Trib. to Clearfield Creek	Ashville, Rt. # 36	2.3 Miles
Ben's Creek	Jamestown, Rt. # 53	2.0 Miles
Bender Run	Carrolltown, Rt. # 219	2.3 Miles
Blacklick Creek North Branch	Belsano, Rt. # 422	7.9 Miles
Chest Creek	Patton, Rt. # 36	13.0 Miles
Clearfield Creek	Cresson, Rt. # 22	2.0 Miles
Conemaugh River, Little, North Branch	Wilmore, Rt. # 53	2.5 Miles
Conemaugh River, South Fork	Lloydell, Rt. # 160	3.0 Miles
Duman Dam	Nicktown, Rt. # 553	20.0 Acres
Elton Sportsmen's Dam	Elton, Rt. # 160	5.0 Acres
Howells Run	Munster, Rt. # 422	4.5 Miles
Killbuck Run	Patton, Rt. # 36	3.0 Miles
Lake Rowena	Ebensburg	11.0 Acres
Laurel Lick Run	Carrolltown, Rt. # 219	2.5 Miles
Laurel Run	Beaverdale, Rt. # 160	2.0 Miles
Laurel Run, Big	Dysart, Rt. # 53	3.5 Miles
Noels Creek	Jamestown, Rt. # 53	3.0 Miles
Paint Creek, Little	Elton, Rt. # 160	2.0 Miles
Slatelick Creek	Fallentimber, Rt. # 53	4.5 Miles
Stewarts Run	Ebensburg, Rts. # 219 & 422	2.0 Miles

NAME OF WATER	MAP REFERENCE TOWN AND HIGHWAY	SIZE
CAMERON		
Brooks Run	Sinnemahoning, Rt. # 120	3.4 Miles
Clear Creek	Emporium, Rt. # 120	7.5 Miles
Cowley Run	Sizerville, # 155	.5 Miles
Driftwood Branch	Driftwood, Rt. # 120	33.0 Miles
Elk Fork	Emporium, Rt. # 120	2.8 Miles
George B. Stevenson Reservoir	Sinnemahoning, Rt. # 120	142.0 Acres
Hicks Run, E. Branch	Driftwood, Rt. # 120	4.0 Miles
Hicks Run, W. Branch	Driftwood, Rt. # 120	2.5 Miles
Hunts Run	Cameron, Rt. # 120	5.0 Miles
Jerry Run, Upper	Sinnemahoning, Rt. # 120	3.8 Miles
Lick Island Run	Sinnemahoning, Rt. # 120	1.6 Miles
Mix Run	Driftwood, Rt. # 120	3.5 Miles
North Creek	Emporium, Rt. # 120	5.5 Miles
Sinnemahoning Creek, First Fork	Sinnemahoning, Rt. # 120	10.0 Miles
Sinnemahoning — Portage Creek	Emporium, Rt. # 120	9.0 Miles
West Creek	Emporium, Rt. # 120	10.5 Miles
Wykoff Run	Sinnemahoning, Rt. # 120	6.0 Miles
CENTRE		
Bald Eagle Creek	Port Matilda, Rt. # 220	29.5 Miles
Beech Creek, South Fork	Snow Shoe, Rt. # 53	4.5 Miles
Benner Run	Unionville, Rt. # 220	1.0 Miles
Big Fill Run	Bald Eagle, Rt. # 220	3.0 Miles
Black Bear Run	Philipsburg, Rt. # 53	4.0 Miles
Black Moshannon Creek	Philipsburg, Rt. # 53	10.5 Miles
Boy Scout Dam	Potters Mills, Rt. # 322	1.2 Acres
Cold Stream Run	Philipsburg, Rt. # 322	3.5 Miles
Dicks Run	Julian, Rt. # 220	3.0 Miles
Eddylick Run	Milesburg, Rt. # 220	5.0 Miles
Elk Creek	Millheim, Rt. # 45	10.8 Miles
Fields Run	Snow Shoe, Rt. # 53	3.0 Miles
Fishing Creek, Little	Mingoville, Rt. # 64	11.5 Miles
Flat Rock Creek	Port Matilda, Rt. # 220	4.0 Miles
Laurel Run (Whetstone)	Julian, Rt. # 220	2.0 Miles
Lick Run	Howard, Rt. # 64	1.3 Miles
Logan Branch	Bellefonte, Rt. # 53	3.0 Miles
Marsh Creek	Blanchard, Rt. # 220	9.0 Miles
McClure Dam	Potters Mills, Rt. # 144	1.0 Acres
Mountain Branch	Houtzdale, Rt. # 53	2.0 Miles
Penns Creek	Spring Mills, Rt. # 45	12.0 Miles
Pine Creek	Woodward, Rt. # 45	6.5 Miles
Poe Creek	Poe Lake, Rt. # 322	3.0 Miles
Poe Lake	Potters Mills, Rt. # 322	24.0 Acres
Rock Run	Snow Shoe, Rt. # 53	2.5 Miles
Sinking Creek	Potters Mills, Rt. # 53	6.0 Miles
Six Mile Run	Phillipsburg, Rt. # 322	6.5 Miles
Spring Creek	Bellefonte, Rt. # 220	15.0 Miles
Spruce Creek	Rock Springs, Rt. # 45	2.0 Miles
Wallace Run	Milesburg, Rt. # 220	2.5 Miles
White Deer Creek	Livonia, Rt. # 95	4.5 Miles
Wolf Run	Snow Shoe, Rt. # 53	4.0 Miles

NAME OF WATER	MAP REFERENCE TOWN AND HIGHWAY	SIZE
CLEARFIELD		
Anderson Creek	Sabula, Rt. # 255	4.5 Miles
Beaver Run	Cherry Tree, Rt. # 219	4.0 Miles
Beech Run	Troutville, Rt. # 410	2.0 Miles
Bennetts Branch, South Branch	Penfield, Rt. # 255	2.5 Miles
Chest Creek	Mahaffey, Rt. # 219	12.0 Miles
Clearfield Creek, Little	Kerrmoor, Rt. # 453	12.7 Miles
Curry Run	Troutville, Rt. # 410	7.0 Miles
Gazzam Branch	New Millport, Rt. # 453	3.5 Miles
Gifford Run	Frenchville, Rt. # 879	4.5 Miles
Goss Run Dam	Brisbin, Rt. # 453	2.0 Acres
Hockenberry Run	Irvona, Rt. # 53	2.5 Miles
Janesville Dam	Janesville, Rt. # 729	10.0 Acres
Laborde Branch	Rockton, Rt. # 410	3.5 Miles
Lick Run	Shawsville, Rt. # 879	4.5 Miles
Medix Run	Penfield, Rt. # 255	4.0 Miles
Mosquito Creek	Frenchville, Rt. # 879	6.5 Miles
North Witmer Run	Irvona, Rt. # 53	3.0 Miles
Parker Lake	Parker Lake, Rt. # 153	20.0 Acres
Sandy Creek	Frenchville, Rt. # 879	4.3 Miles
Sawmill Run	Burnside, Rt. # 219	2.0 Miles
Sinnemahoning Creek, Bennetts Branch	Penfield, Rt. # 255	3.3 Miles
South Witmer Run	Irvona, Rt. # 53	4.0 Miles
Stone Run	Clearfield, Rt. # 322	3.0 Miles
Tannery Dam (Juniata Lake)	DuBois, Rt. # 219	5.0 Acres
Trout Run	Shawsville, Rt. # 879	9.0 Miles
Muddy Run, Little	Janesville, Rt. # 729	5.0 Miles

Small streams present the best challenge to the fly fisherman. However, clear, low waters create difficult conditions, especially at midday. Note the concentration by this angler.

46

NAME OF WATER	MAP REFERENCE TOWN AND HIGHWAY	SIZE
CLINTON		
Baker Run	Glen Union, Rt. # 220	4.0 Miles
Beaverdam Run	Hammersley Fork, Rt. # 144	2.2 Miles
Birch Island Run	Pottersdale, Leg. Rt. # 17068	1.5 Miles
Cooks Run	Westport, Rt. # 120	4.0 Miles
Fishing Creek, Big	Lamar, Rt. # 220	21.0 Miles
Hammersley Fork	Hammersley Fork, Rt. # 144	2.5 Miles
Hyner Run	Hyner, Rt. # 120	8.5 Miles
Hyner Run, Left Branch	Hyner, Rt. # 120	1.8 Miles
Kettle Creek	Hammersley Fork, Rt. # 144	17.5 Miles
Kettle Creek Lake	Renovo, Rt. # 120	160.0 Acres
Long Run	Salona, Rt. # 880	3.5 Miles
Paddy Run	Renovo, Rt. # 120	3.0 Miles
Shingle Branch	North Bend, Rt. # 120	6.0 Miles
Tangascootack Creek, North Fork	Lock Haven, Rt. # 220	4.0 Miles
Trout Run	Hammersley Fork, Rt. # 144	2.5 Miles
Young Woman's Creek	North Bend, Rt. # 120	2.3 Miles
Young Woman's Creek, Left Branch	North Bend, Rt. # 120	12.0 Miles
Young Woman's Creek, Right Branch	North Bend, Rt. # 120	8.5 Miles
Rouchtown Creek (Antes Creek)	Rouchtown, Rt. # 880	3.0 Miles
CUMBERLAND		
Big Spring Creek	Newville, Rt. # 233	3.2 Miles
Boiling Springs Lake	Boiling Springs, Rt. # 174	9.0 Acres
Fuller Lake	Pine Grove Furnace State Park, Rt. # 233	1.7 Acres
Green Spring Creek	Newville, Rt. # 641	2.0 Miles
Laurel Lake	Mt. Holly Springs, Rt. # 34	25.0 Acres
Letort Spring Run	Carlisle, Rt. # 11	1.7 Miles
Middle Spring Creek	Shippensburg, Rt. # 11	5.0 Miles
Mountain Creek	Pine Grove Furnace, Rt. # 233	15.0 Miles
Old Town Run	Boiling Springs, Rt. # 174	2.0 Miles
Opossum Creek Lake	Plainfield, Rt. # 641	60.0 Acres
Yellow Breeches Creek	Huntsdale, Rt. # 233	38.5 Miles
Doubling Gap Lake	Doubling Gap, Rt. # 233	4.0 Acres
ELK		
Bear Creek	Owls Nest Oil Station	15.0 Miles
Bear Run	Brockport, Rt. # 219	2.0 Miles
Belmuth Run	Ridgway, Rt. # 219	2.5 Miles
Boggy Run	Brockport, Rt. # 219	3.0 Miles
Byrnes Run	Kersey, Rt. # 948	3.5 Miles
Clarion River, East Branch	Elk Park, East, Rt. # 219	5.0 Miles
Clarion River, West Branch	St. Marys, Rt. # 255	10.0 Miles
Crooked Creek	St. Marys, Rt. # 255	3.0 Miles
Driftwood Branch	Lockwood, Rt. # 46	2.5 Miles
Hicks Run	Driftwood, Rt. # 120	2.0 Miles
Hicks Run, East Branch	Driftwood, Rt. # 120	2.5 Miles
Hicks Run, West Branch	Medix Run, Rt. # 555	3.5 Miles
Hoffman Run	Dahaga, Rt. # 219	4.0 Miles
Laurel Run	Ridgway, Rt. # 219	2.5 Miles
Maxwell Run	Ridgway, Rt. # 219	3.0 Miles
Medix Run	Medix Run, Rt. # 555	3.0 Miles
Middle Fork	St. Marys, Rt. # 255	3.0 Miles
Mill Creek, Big	Bridge on Route # 948	15.0 Miles

NAME OF WATER	MAP REFERENCE TOWN AND HIGHWAY	SIZE
ELK CO. (con't.)		
Millstone Creek, East Branch	Loleta Camping Area	11.0 Miles
Mix Run	Driftwood, Rt. # 120	3.8 Miles
Powers Run	St. Marys, Rt. # 255	2.0 Miles
Red Run	Curtis-Wright Corp., Rt. # 879	2.4 Miles
Ridgway Reservoir	Ridgway, Rt. # 219	75.0 Acres
Rocky Run	Wilcox, Rt. # 219	3.0 Miles
Spring Creek	Russell City, Rts. # 68 & 948	11.0 Miles
Spring Creek, East Branch	Russell City, Rts. # 68 & 948	12.0 Miles
Spring Run	Bryndale Hill, Rt. # 555	2.0 Miles
Straight Creek	Clermont, Rt. # 146	2.0 Miles
Straight Creek, South Fork	Clermont, Rt. # 146	2.0 Miles
Twin Lakes	Dahaga, Rt. # 219	7.5 Acres
Vineyard Run	Ridgway, Rt. # 219	2.5 Miles
West Creek	St. Marys, Rt. # 255	3.0 Miles
Wilson Run	Wilcox, Rt. # 219	8.0 Miles
Wolf Lick Run	Kersey, Rt. # 948	4.0 Miles
Wolf Run	Russell City, Rts. # 68 & 948	6.0 Miles
East Branch Clarion River Lake	Elk Park, East, Rt. #219	1160.0 Acres
Laurel Run Reservoir	St. Marys, Rt. # 120	100.0 Acres
FRANKLIN		
Antietam Creek, East Branch	Waynesboro, Rt. # 16	11.0 Miles
Antietam Creek, West Branch	Waynesboro, Rt. # 16	11.0 Miles
Broad Run	Fort Loudon, Rt. # 30	4.5 Miles
Campbell Run	St. Thomas, Rt. # 30	2.0 Miles
Carbaugh Run	Caledonia State Park, Rt. # 30	1.0 Miles
Conococheague Creek	Chambersburg, Rt. # 11	21.0 Miles
Conococheague Creek, West Branch	Fort Loudon, Rt. # 30	20.0 Miles
Conodoguinet Creek	Bear Valley State Park	9.0 Miles
Cove Creek, Little	Mercersburg, Rt. # 16	6.5 Miles
Dennis Creek	Chambersburg, Rt. # 11	2.5 Miles
Dickeys Run	Mercersburg, Rt. # 16	2.0 Miles
Falling Spring Branch	Staufferstown, Rt. # 30	5.1 Miles
Five Forks Creek	Waynesboro, Rt. # 16	2.5 Miles
Letterkenny Reservoir	Roxbury, Rt. # 641	54.0 Miles
Muddy Run	Greencastle, Rt. # 16	5.0 Miles
Red Run	Waynesboro, Rt. # 16	2.0 Miles
Roe Run	Orrstown, Rt. # 433	2.0 Miles
FULTON		
Aughwick Creek, Little	McConnellsburg, Rt. # 30	7.5 Miles
Aughwick Creek, Little, South Branch	McConnellsburg, Rt. # 30	11.0 Miles
Barnetts Run	Needmore, Rt. # 522	3.0 Miles
Brush Creek	Crystal Springs, Rt. # 126	7.5 Miles
Brush Creek, Little	Crystal Springs, Rt. # 126	6.2 Miles
Cove Creek	McConnellsburg, Rt. # 30	11.5 Miles
Cowan's Gap Lake	McConnellsburg, Rt. # 30	42.0 Acres
Laurel Fork Creek	Wells Tannery, Rt. # 915	2.0 Miles
Licking Creek	McConnellsburg, Rt. # 30	9.0 Miles
Nine Mile Creek	Burnt Cabins, Rt. # 522	1.5 Miles
Oregon Creek	Wells Tannery, Rt. # 915	3.0 Miles

A Pennsylvania Fish Commission patrolman posts the regulations pertaining to fly fishing only waters. When you see these posters take a moment to read the rules.

NAME OF WATER	MAP REFERENCE TOWN AND HIGHWAY	SIZE
FULTON CO. (con't.)		
Roaring Run. Trib. to Little Brush Creek	Crystal Springs, Rt. # 126	2.0 Miles
Roaring Run. Trib. to Cove Creek	McConnellsburg, Rt. # 30	4.5 Miles
Sideling Hill Creek	Wells Tannery, Rt. # 915	5.0 Miles
Spring Run	Websters Mills, Rt. # 522	2.5 Miles
Tonoloway Creek, Little	Warfordsburg, Rt. # 522	10.0 Miles
Wooden Bridge Creek	Hustontown, Rt. # 176	8.0 Miles

FISHING GUIDES

CANOEING & FISHING UPPER DELAWARE R.	PENNSYLVANIA TROUT	CATSKILL TROUT	NEW JERSEY TROUT
$5.95	**$5.95**	**$5.95**	**$5.95**

Pathfinder Publications offers four excellent fishing guides, detailing streams, locations, lures, methods, and much more, fully illustrated with maps and photos. A handy 6x9 softcover that easily fits your jacket or tackle box. An excellent reference when planning your trip.

Already available at many dealers or you may order by mail. When ordering please add 75¢ postage, N.J. residents add 5% tax. **DEALER INQUIRY WELCOME.**

PATHFINDER PUBLICATIONS INC.
210 CENTRAL AVENUE, MADISON, NEW JERSEY 07940

The smile tells the story, a beautiful opening day brownie, and a very happy youngster.

NAME OF WATER	MAP REFERENCE TOWN AND HIGHWAY	SIZE
HUNTINGDON		
Barree Dam	Barree, Rt. # 115	3.5 Acres
Blacklog Creek	Orbisonia, Rt. # 522	14.5 Miles
Garners Run	Neffs Mills, Rt. # 305	2.5 Miles
Globe Run	Neffs Mills, Rt. # 305	4.5 Miles
Great Trough Creek	Marklesburg, Rt. # 26	3.5 Miles
Greenwood Lake	Greenwood Furnace, Rt. # 305	3.0 Acres
Laurel Run	McAlveys Fort, Rt. # 545	8.0 Miles
Nine Mile Creek	Burnt Cabins, Rt. # 522	2.5 Miles
North Spring Branch	Saltillo, Rt. # 76	4.5 Miles
Saddler Creek	Mill Creek, Rt. # 76	5.0 Miles
Shade Creek	Orbisonia, Rt. # 522	3.3 Miles
Shavers Creek	Neffs Mills, Rt. # 305	8.0 Miles
Shavers Lake (Stone Valley Lake)	Neffs Mills, Rt. # 305	75.0 Acres
Standing Stone Creek	McAlveys Fort, Rt. # 545	27.5 Miles
Standing Stone Creek, East Branch	Cornpropst Mills, Rt. # 545	8.5 Miles
Three Springs Creek	Saltillo, Rt. # 76	3.9 Miles
Tuscarora Creek	Blairs Mills, Rt. # 829	6.0 Miles
West Licking Creek	Mt. Union, Rt. # 22	4.0 Miles
Whipple Lake	McAlveys Fort, Rt. # 545	22.0 Acres
JUNIATA		
Big Run	Mifflintown, Rt. # 322	3.0 Miles
Blacklog Creek	Shade Gap, Rt. # 522	3.5 Miles
Cocolamus Creek	Cocolamus, Rt. # 35	9.0 Miles
Delaware Creek	Thompsontown, Rt. # 22	3.0 Miles
Horning Run	Mifflintown, Rt. # 322	3.5 Miles
Horse Valley Run	East Waterford, Rt. # 75	2.0 Miles
Liberty Valley Run	Honey Grove, Rt. # 75	2.0 Miles
Licking Creek	Mifflintown, Rt. # 22	10.5 Miles
Lost Creek	McAllisterville, Rt. # 35	11.0 Miles
Tuscarora Creek	East Waterford, Rt. # 75	9.5 Miles
Willow Run	Honey Grove, Rt. # 75	8.0 Miles

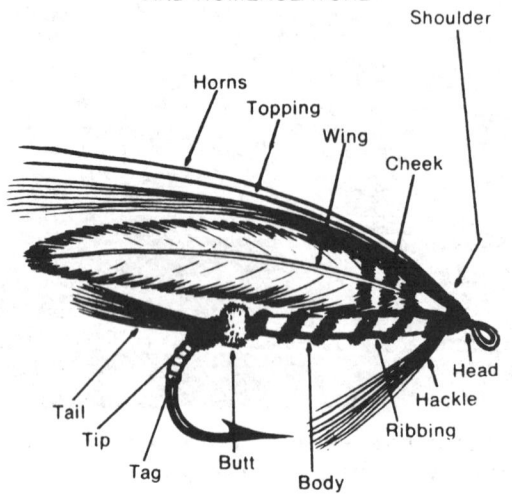

TYPICAL FLY AND NOMENCLATURE

NAME OF WATER	MAP REFERENCE TOWN AND HIGHWAY	SIZE
LYCOMING		
Bear Creek, Little	Loyalsockville, Rt. # 87	4.0 Miles
Black Hole Creek	Montgomery, Rt. # 14	4.1 Miles
Blockhouse Run	English Center, Rt. # 84	6.2 Miles
Grays Run	Fields Station, Rt. # 14	4.0 Miles
Hogland Run	Cogan Station, Rt. # 111	6.0 Miles
Larry's Creek	Salladasburg, Rt. # 84	6.5 Miles
Little Pine Lake	Waterville, Rt. # 44	90.0 Acres
Loyalsock Creek	Loyalsock, Rt. # 87	14.5 Miles
Lycoming Creek	Cogan Station, Rt. # 15	21.5 Miles
Mill Creek, West	Montoursville, Rt. # 111	5.5 Miles
Muncy Creek	Muncy, Rt. # 220	13.5 Miles
Muncy Creek, Little	Lairdsville, Rt. # 642	5.0 Miles
Pine Bottom Run, Upper	Waterville, Rt. # 44	3.5 Miles
Pine Creek	Waterville, Rt. # 44	24.0 Miles
Pine Creek, Little	Waterville, Rt. # 44	12.0 Miles
Pleasant Stream	Marsh Hill, Rt. # 14	9.5 Miles
Roaring Run	Roaring Branch, Rt. # 14	2.0 Miles
Rock Run, Trib. to Lycoming Crook	Ralston, Rt. # 14	5.0 Miles
Slate Run	Slate Run, Rt. # 893	6.5 Miles
Spring Creek	Elimsport, Rt. # 44	4.0 Miles
Trout Run. Trib. to Pine Creek	Pump Station, Rt. # 44	5.0 Miles
Wallis Run	Loyalsockville, Rt. # 87	5.0 Miles
White Deer Hole Creek	Elimsport, Rt. # 44	10.9 Miles
McKEAN		
Allegheny River	Port Allegany, Rt. # 6	5.0 Miles
Allegheny-Portage Creek	Port Allegany, Rt. # 6	2.0 Miles
Bell Run	Shinglehouse, Rt. # 44	2.5 Miles
Brewer Run	Betula, Rt. # 46	1.8 Miles
Chappel Fork	Marshburg, Rt. # 59	9.0 Miles
Clarion River, West Branch	Halsey, Rt. # 219	5.0 Miles
Colegrove Brook	Colegrove, Rt. # 46	1.8 Miles
Combs Creek	Port Allegany, Rt. # 6	3.0 Miles
Havens Run	Betula, Rt. # 46	2.0 Miles
Kinzua Creek	Westline, off Rt. # 219	23.0 Miles
Kinzua Creek, South Branch	Kane, Rt. # 6	15.0 Miles
Lewis Run	Lewis Run, Rt. # 219	6.0 Miles
Marvin Creek	Smethport, Rt. # 6	11.5 Miles
Potato Creek	Crosby, Rt. # 46	16.0 Miles
Potato Creek, West Branch	Smethport, Rt. # 6	4.0 Miles
Seven Mile Run	Wilcox, Rt. # 219	3.5 Miles
Skinner Creek	Port Allegany, Rt. # 6	4.5 Miles
Sugar Run	Junction of Rts. # 59 & 346	8.0 Miles
Sugar Run, North Branch	Junction of Rts. # 59 & 346	5.0 Miles
Tionesta Creek, East Branch	Kane, Rt. # 6	16.0 Miles
Tunungwant Creek, East Branch	Lewis Run, Rt. # 219	12.0 Miles
Willow Creek	Corydon, Rt. # 346	10.0 Miles

Hundreds of fishable streams offer many solitary places where the angler can find peace of mind as well as a few trout.

NAME OF WATER	MAP REFERENCE TOWN AND HIGHWAY	SIZE
MIFFLIN		
Havice Creek	Seiglerville, Rt. # 983	5.5 Miles
Honey Creek	Milroy, Rt. # 322	13.5 Miles
Kishacoquillas Creek	Reedsville, Rt. # 322	11.0 Miles
Licking Creek	Mifflintown, Rt. # 322	6.0 Miles
Lingle Run	Milroy, Rt. # 322	5.5 Miles
Meadow Creek	Alfarata, Rt. # 522	3.5 Miles
Messer Run	McVeytown, Rt. # 22	3.0 Miles
Penns Creek	Milroy, Rt. # 322	2.0 Miles
Strodes Run	Strodes Mill, Rt. # 522	2.6 Miles
Tea Creek	Reedsville, Rt. # 322	1.0 Miles
Town Run	McVeytown, Rt. # 22	2.0 Miles
Treaster Run	Lockes Mills, Rt. # 972	5.5 Miles
West Licking Creek	Mt. Union, Rt. # 22	1.5 Miles
PERRY		
Bixler Run	Loysville, Rt. # 274	4.0 Miles
Buffalo Creek	Ickesburg, Rt. # 17	16.0 Miles
Buffalo Creek, Little	Newport, Rt. # 34	3.0 Miles
Fishing Creek	Marysville, Rts. # 11 & 15	4.5 Miles
Fowler Hollow Run	Blain, Rt. # 274	1.7 Miles
Horse Valley Run	East Waterford, Rt. # 75	4.5 Miles
Juniata Creek, Little	New Bloomfield, Rt. # 34	9.5 Miles
Laurel Run	Landisburg, Rt. # 850	13.5 Miles
Liberty Valley Run	Honey Grove, Rt. # 75	3.5 Miles
Montour Run	Landisburg, Rt. # 850	4.0 Miles
Panther Creek	Ickesburg, Rt. # 74	3.0 Miles
Raccoon Creek	Ickesburg, Rt. # 74	8.0 Miles
Shaffer Run	Blain, Rt. # 274	8.0 Miles
Sherman Creek	Blain, Rt. # 274	17.0 Miles
Shultz Creek (Browns Run)	Blain, Rt. # 274	4.0 Miles
POTTER		
Allegheny River	Durtville, Rt. # 6	15.5 Miles
Bailey Run	Sinnemahoning, Rt. # 872	1.5 Miles
Bell Run	Shinglehouse, Rt. # 44	2.0 Miles
Cowanesque River	Westfield, Rt. # 449	1.0 Miles
Cowley Creek, East Branch	Sizerville, Rt. # 155	3.3 Miles
Cowley Creek, West Branch	Sizerville, Rt. # 155	2.5 Miles
Cross Fork Creek	Cross Forks, Rt. # 144	9.5 Miles
Dingman Run	Coudersport, Rt. # 6	2.5 Miles
Dry Run	Sweden Valley, Rt. # 6	1.5 Miles
Eleven Mile Creek	Millsport, Rt. # 44	3.4 Miles
Fishing Creek	Roulette, Rt. # 6	1.8 Miles
Fishing Creek, East Branch	Roulette, Rt. # 6	2.5 Miles
Fishing Creek, West Branch	Roulette, Rt. # 6	3.0 Miles
Freeman Run	Costello, Rt. # 872	7.5 Miles
Freeman Run, West Branch	Austin, Rts. # 872 & 607	2.5 Miles
Genesee River	Genesee, Rt. # 449	5.0 Miles

NAME OF WATER	MAP REFERENCE TOWN AND HIGHWAY	SIZE
Genesee River, Middle Branch	Genesee, Rt. # 449	7.5 Miles
Genesee River, West Branch	Genesee, Rt. # 449	4.5 Miles
Kettle Creek	Cross Forks, Rt. # 144	17.5 Miles
Kettle Creek, Germania Branch	Germania, Rt. # 144	2.0 Miles
Kettle Creek, Little	Oleona, Rt. # 44	5.5 Miles
Ludington Branch	Genesee, Rt. # 449	3.0 Miles
Lyman Run	Galeton, Rt. # 6	6.5 Miles
Lyman Lake	Galeton, Rt. # 6	40.0 Acres
Mill Creek	Coudersport, Rt. # 6	5.5 Miles
Moore Run, Big	Costello, Rt. # 872	3.3 Miles
Nine Mile Run	Galeton, Rt. # 6	3.5 Miles
Oswayo Creek	Sharon Center, Rt. # 44	9.3 Miles
Oswayo Creek, South Branch	Coneville, Rt. # 44	3.3 Miles
Pine Creek	Galeton, Rt. # 6	12.4 Miles
Pine Creek, Genesee Fork	Westpike, Rt. # 6	9.0 Miles
Pine Creek, West Branch	Galeton, Rt. # 6	12.5 Miles
Prouty Branch	Costello, Rts. # 872 & 52002	3.0 Miles
Reed Run	Roulette, Rt. # 6	1.8 Miles
Reynoldstown Branch	Ellisburg, Rt. # 244	2.0 Miles
Sartwell Creek	Burtville, Rt. # 6	3.5 Miles
Sinnemahoning Creek, First Fork	Wharton, Rt. # 872	19.0 Miles
Sinnemahoning Creek, East Fork of First Fork	Wharton, Rt. # 872	12.0 Miles
Sinnemahoning Creek, South Branch of First Fork	Costello, Rt. # 872	6.0 Miles

SNYDER

Kern (Kuhn-Hoover) Run	Beavertown, Rt. # 522	2.8 Miles
Krepp Gap Run	Troxelville, Rt. # 929	2.0 Miles
Mahantango Creek, North Branch	Mt. Pleasant Mills, Rt. # 104	4.5 Miles
Mahantango Creek, West Branch	Richfield, Rt. # 35	4.0 Miles
Middle Creek	Beavertown, Rt. # 522	14.9 Miles
Middle Creek, North Branch	Troxelville, Rt. # 929	2.6 Miles
Middle Creek, West Branch	McClure, Rt. # 522	4.3 Miles
Swift Run	Troxelville, Rt. # 929	6.6 Miles

TIOGA

Asaph Run	Ansonia, Rt. # 6	4.3 Miles
Bailey Creek	Mansfield, Rt. # 549	3.0 Miles
Beechwood Lake	Sabinsville, Rt. # 349	67.0 Acres
Black Creek	Liberty, Rt. # 15	2.4 Miles
Cedar Run	Cedar Run, Rt. # 893	7.0 Miles

Bridges always attract anglers, and rightly so since bridges and surrounding waters nearly always hold a large number of trout.

NAME OF WATER	MAP REFERENCE TOWN AND HIGHWAY	SIZE
Cowanesque River	Westfield, Rt. # 449	3.0 Miles
Elk Run	Galeton, Rt. # 6	5.0 Miles
Kettle Creek	Gaines, Rt. # 6	2.3 Miles
Lake Hamilton	Wellsboro, Rt. # 6	42.0 Acres
Long Run, Trib. to Babbs Creek	Morris, Rt. # 85	2.0 Miles
Long Run, Trib. to Pine Creek	Gaines, Rt. # 6	4.0 Miles
Marsh Creek	Ansonia, Rt. # 6	2.0 Miles
Mill Creek	Mansfield, Rt. # 15	11.6 Miles
Mill Creek, West Branch	Roaring Branch, Rt. # 14	3.5 Miles
Phoenix Run	Galeton, Rt. # 6	3.5 Miles
Pine Creek	Ansonia, Rt. # 6	19.5 Miles
Roaring Run	Roaring Branch, Rt. # 14	2.5 Miles
Seeley Creek	Mosherville, Rt. # 549	2.5 Miles
Slate Run	Slate Run, Rt. # 893	3.0 Miles
Stony Fork Creek	Stony Fork, Rt. # 960	4.0 Miles
Straight Run	Marsh Creek, Rt. # 6	2.0 Miles
Tioga River	Blossburg, Rt. # 15	0.1 Miles
Stony Fork Creek, East Branch	Stony Fork, Rt. # 960	2.7 Miles

NAME OF WATER	MAP REFERENCE TOWN AND HIGHWAY	SIZE
UNION		
Bear Run	Laurelton, Rt. # 888	2.0 Miles
Buffalo Creek	Mifflinburg, Rt. # 45	10.0 Miles
Buffalo Creek, Little	West Milton, Rt. # 404	2.0 Miles
Buffalo Creek, North Branch	Mifflinburg, Rt. # 45	8.5 Miles
Cherry Run	Laurelton, Rt. # 888	2.5 Miles
Halfway Lake	Livonia, Rt. # 95	7.0 Acres
Laurel Run	Laurelton, Rt. # 888	6.0 Miles
Penns Creek	Laurelton, Rt. # 888	11.0 Miles
Rapid Run	Cowan, Rt. # 95	12.0 Miles
Spring Creek	Elimsport, Rt. # 44	2.5 Miles
Spruce Run	Mifflinburg, Rt. # 45	8.5 Miles
Weikert Run	Laurelton, Rt. # 888	2.5 Miles
White Deer Creek	White Deer, Rt. # 975	19.0 Miles
YORK		
Beaver Run	Windsor, Rt. # 624	2.0 Miles
Blymire Hollow Run	Wintertown, Rt. # 24	2.0 Miles
Codorus Creek	Sinsheim, Rt. # 516	2.5 Miles
Codorus Creek, East Branch	Jacobus, Rt. # 111	4.0 Miles
Fishing Creek, Trib. to Susquehanna River	Windsor, Rt. # 624	5.0 Miles
Fishing Creek, Trib. to Susquehanna River	Goldsboro, Rt. # 920	3.0 Miles
Furnace Run	York Furnace, Rt. # 124	2.0 Miles
Haldeman Pond No. 1	Hanover, Rt. # 94	8.0 Acres
Haldeman Pond No. 2	Spring Grove, Rt. # 116	2.0 Acres
Muddy Creek	Red Lion, Rt. # 74	12.0 Miles
Muddy Creek, North Branch	Red Lion, Rt. # 74	7.0 Miles
Muddy Creek, South Branch	Red Lion, Rt. # 74	7.6 Miles
Otter Creek	New Bridgeville, Rt. # 124	9.4 Miles
Reymayer Hollow Run	Jacobus, Rt. # 111	2.0 Miles
Toms Run	Red Lion, Rt. # 74	2.0 Miles
Wallace Run	Kyleville, Rt. # 74	2.0 Miles
Bald Eagle Creek	Woodbine, Rt. # 425	2.0 Miles
Codorus Creek, West Branch	Spring Grove, Rt. # 516	4.0 Miles

September is an excellent time for trout fishing in Pennsylvania and many rainbow trout of above average size are commonly taken by fly fishermen and bait anglers.

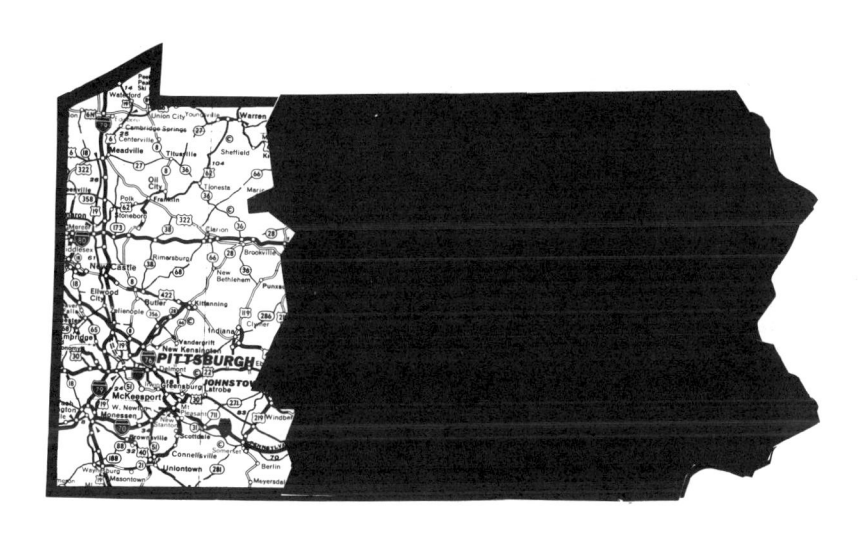

WESTERN REGION

COUNTIES

Allegheny, Armstrong, Beaver, Butler, Clarion, Crawford, Erie, Fayette, Forest, Greene, Indiana, Jefferson, Lawrence, Mercer, Somerset, Venango, Warren, Washington, Westmoreland.

NAME OF WATER	MAP REFERENCE TOWN AND HIGHWAY	SIZE
ALLEGHENY		
Bull Creek	Millerstown, Rt. # 28	5.8 Miles
Deer Creek, Big	Indianola, Rt. # 910	8.0 Miles
Flaugherty Run	Cornot, Rt. # 51	2.0 Miles
Long Run (Jack's Run)	White Oak Boro	2.7 Miles
North Park Lake	Warrendale, Rt. # 19	74.0 Acres
Pine Creek	North Park Lake, Rt. # 8	2.0 Miles
Pucketa Creek	New Kensington, Rt. # 366	4.0 Miles
Sewickley Creek	Pinehurst, Rt. # 820	4.1 Miles
ARMSTRONG		
Buffalo Creek	Boggsville, Rt. # 228	13.8 Miles
Cherry Run	Elderton, Rt. # 422	5.0 Miles
Cornplanter Run	Boggsville, Rt. # 228	2.0 Miles
Glade Run	Cowansville, Rt. # 268	7.6 Miles
Huling Run	Cowansville, Rt. # 268	2.8 Miles
Patterson Creek	Worthington, Rt. # 422	5.2 Miles
Pine Creek, North Fork	Kittanning, Rt. # 422	5.0 Miles
Pine Creek, South Fork (North Branch)	Yatesboro, Rt. # 85	3.5 Miles
Pine Creek, South Fork	Kittanning, Rt. # 422	9.5 Miles
Plum Creek	Gastown, Rt. # 210	4.5 Miles
Scrubgrass Creek	Kittanning, Rt. # 422	5.0 Miles

BEAVER

Beaver River, Little North Fork	Darlington, Rt. # 151	4.5 Miles
Brady Run Lake	Rochester, Rt. # 68	41.0 Acres
Brady Run, South Branch	Rochester, Rt. # 18	2.8 Miles
Hereford Manor Lake, Lower	Zelienople, N. Rt. # 288	45.0 Acres
Hereford Manor Lake, Upper	Zelienople, N. Rt. # 288	27.0 Acres
Mill Creek	Hookstown, Rt. # 168	3.5 Miles
Raccoon Lake	Frankfort Springs, Rt. # 18	101.0 Acres
Sewickley Creek, North Fork	Economy, Rt. # 65	2.0 Miles
Traverse Creek, Big	Frankfort Springs, Rt. # 18	3.5 Miles

BUTLER

Bear Creek	Bruin, Rt. # 268	7.0 Miles
Buffalo Creek	Millerstown, Rt. # 68	7.0 Miles
Buffalo Run, Little	Butler, Rt. # 422	2.5 Miles
Connoquenessing Creek, Little	Butler, Rt. # 68	4.0 Miles
Game Lands, No. 95, Lake No. 5	Boyers, Rt. # 308	1.0 Acres
Harber Acres Lake	West Sunbury	15.0 Acres
McMurray Run	Harrisville, Rt. # 8	2.5 Miles
Silver Creek	Bruin, Rt. # 268	3.5 Miles
Slippery Rock Creek	Stone House, Rt. # 8 & 173	6.8 Miles
Slippery Rock Creek, North Branch	Harrisville, Rt. # 8	6.5 Miles
Thorn Creek	Butler, Rt. # 8	5.5 Miles

CLARION

Beaver Creek	Knox, Rt. # 238	3.0 Miles
Canoe Creek	Knox, Rt. # 208	2.5 Miles
Cathers Run	Cook State Forest, Rt. # 36	2.0 Miles
East Sandy Creek	Van. Rt. # 322	3.0 Miles
Leatherwood Creek	Curllsville, Rt. # 854	5.0 Miles
Mill Creek	Clarion, Rt. # 322	3.0 Miles
Turkey Run	Turkey City, Rt. # 338	3.0 Miles
Ritchey Run	Emlenton, Rt. # 38	2.5 Miles

CRAWFORD

Caldwell Creek	Grand Valley Rt. # 27	2.0 Miles
Conneaut Creek	Springboro, Rt. # 18	10.0 Miles
Five Mile Creek	Spartanburg, Rt. # 77	2.0 Miles
McLaughlin Creek	Hydetown, Rt. # 8	3.7 Miles
Muddy Creek	Little Cooley, Rt. # 77	9.0 Miles
Oil Creek	Centerville, Rt. # 8	19.1 Miles
Oil Creek, East Branch	Centerville, Rt. # 8	9.9 Miles
Pine Creek	Titusville, Rt. # 36	2.0 Miles
Shirley Run	Hydetown, Rt. # 8	2.0 Miles
Sugar Creek	Titusville, Rt. # 27	4.0 Miles
Sugar Creek, East Branch	Troy Center, Rt. # 428	3.5 Miles
Sugar Creek, Little	Cochranton, Rt. # 322	10.0 Miles
Thompson Run	Hydetown, Rt. # 8	3.5 Miles
Woodcock Creek	Saegertown, Rt. # 6	9.0 Miles

NAME OF WATER	MAP REFERENCE TOWN AND HIGHWAY	SIZE
ERIE		
Beaver (Beaverdam) Run	Corry, Rt. # 6	4.7 Miles
Conneauttee Creek	Edinboro, Rt. # 99	4.0 Miles
Conneauttee Creek, Little	Edinboro, Rt. # 99	2.3 Miles
Crooked Creek	Route # 5	6.0 Miles
Elk Creek	Girard, Rt. # 20	5.0 Miles
French Creek	Wattsburg, Rt. # 89	3.9 Miles
French Creek, South Branch	Union City, Rt. # 8	7.0 Miles
Hatch Hollow Run	Wattsburg, Rt. # 8	3.0 Miles
Lake Pleasant	Arbuckle, Rt. # 8	60.0 Acres
LeBoeuf Creek	Waterford, Rt. # 19	5.5 Miles
LeBoeuf Creek, East Branch	Waterford, Rt. # 19	3.6 Miles
Trout (Boyd's) Run	Waterford, Rt. # 19	2.5 Miles
Twenty Mile Creek	Northeast, Rt. # 20	2.0 Miles

A Game Commission employee is on the scene to assist this youngster in landing his first rainbow trout.

NAME OF WATER	TOWN AND HIGHWAY	SIZE
FAYETTE		
Back Creek	Indian Head, Rt. # 711	2.8 Miles
Chaney Run	Hopwood, Rt. # 40	3.0 Miles
Dunbar Creek	Dunbar, Rt. # 119	6.0 Miles
Dunlap Creek Flood Control Reservoir # 2	Brownsville, Rt. # 40	50.0 Acres
Indian Creek	Melcroft, Rt. # 711	4.8 Miles
Jonathan Run	Ohiopyle, Rt. # 381	2.0 Miles
Meadow Run, Big	Ohiopyle, Rt. # 381	12.5 Miles
Mill Run, Trib. to Indian Creek	Indian Head, Rt. # 711	3.0 Miles
Mill Run, Trib. to Big Sandy Creek	Elliotsville, Rt. # 383	6.0 Miles
Mountain Creek	Smithfield, Rt. # 119	2.6 Miles
Sandy Creek, Big	Elliottsville, Rt. # 381	5.0 Miles
Virgin Run Dam	Perryopolis, Rt. # 51	35.0 Acres

NAME OF WATER	MAP REFERENCE TOWN AND HIGHWAY	SIZE
FOREST		
Beaver Creek	Endeavor, Rt. # 666	8.0 Miles
Bluejay Creek	Lynch Bridge, Rt. # 666	7.0 Miles
Coon Creek, Little	Marienville, Rt. # 68	3.0 Miles
Hickory Creek, East	Endeavor, Rt. # 666	16.0 Miles
Hickory Creek, Little	East Hickory, Rt. # 62	4.0 Miles
Hickory Creek, West	West Hickory, Rt. # 127	6.0 Miles
Maple Creek	Marienville, Rt. # 68	4.0 Miles
Millstone Creek, West Branch	Marienville, Rt. # 68	15.0 Miles
Salmon Creek	Marienville, Rt. # 68	17.0 Miles
Tionesta Creek	Tionesta, Rt. # 62	17.0 Miles
Toms Run	Cooksbury (in Cook Forest)	4.9 Miles
Ward's Ranch Pond	Vowinckel, Rt. # 68	10.0 Acres
GREENE		
Ryerson Station Lake	Wind Ridge, Rt. # 21	61.0 Acres
Wheeling Creek, Dunkard Fork	Wind Ridge, Rt. # 21	2.5 Miles
Wheeling Creek, N.F., Dunkard Fork	Wind Ridge, Rt. # 21	2.0 Miles
Wheeling Creek, S.F., Dunkard Fork	Wind Ridge, Rt. # 21	3.6 Miles
INDIANA		
Brush Creek	Blacklick, Rt. # 56	4.0 Miles
Cush-Cushion Creek	Cherry Tree, Rt. # 219	2.5 Miles
Laurel Run, Trib. to Yellow Creek, Big	Nolo. Rt. #236	4.0 Miles
Mahoning Creek, Little	Rochester Mills, Rt. # 236	22.0 Miles
Mudlick Run	Rochester Mills, Rt. # 236	3.0 Miles
Twolick Creek, South Branch	Pine Flats, Rt. # 480	6.0 Miles
Yellow Creek	Ewing Mills, Rt. # 422	6.5 Miles
Yellow Creek, Little	Strongtown, Rt. # 422	7.5 Miles
JEFFERSON		
Big Run, Trib. to Mahoning Creek	Cramer, Rt. # 925	2.0 Miles
Big Run, Trib. to Sandy Creek, Little	Sprankle Mills, Rt. # 36 & 536	4.5 Miles
Callen Run	Brookville, Rt. # 36	2.5 Miles
Cathers Run	Brookville, Rt. # 322	2.5 Miles
Clear Creek	Sigel, Rt. # 36	2.5 Miles
Clear Run	Sigel, Rt. # 36	2.8 Miles
Cloe Dam	Big Run, Rt. # 119	30.0 Acres
Horm Run	Emericksville, Rt. # 322	2.5 Miles
Mahoning Creek, East Branch	Big Run, Rt. # 119	5.5 Miles
Mill Creek, Trib. to Sandylick Creek	Brookville, Rt. # 322	10.0 Miles
Mill Creek, Little	Brookville, Rt. # 322	3.0 Miles
Pekin Run	Brookville, Rt. # 322	3.5 Miles
Rattlesnake Creek	Lanes Mills, Rt. # 219	2.8 Miles
Red Bank Creek	Baxter, Rt. # 28	12.5 Miles
Red Bank Creek, North Fork	Brockway, Rt. # 219	18.0 Miles
Sandy Creek, Little	Punxsutawney, Rt. # 119	11.0 Miles
Walburn Run. W. Br.	Brockway, Rt. # 219	2.0 Miles
Wolf Creek	DuBois, Rt. # 219	2.3 Miles
Rattlesnake Run	Brockway, Rt. # 119	2.5 Miles

Low water time in hot weather will still produce plenty of trout. Of course you will need a bit more patience, and offer the correct fly pattern.

NAME OF WATER	MAP REFERENCE TOWN AND HIGHWAY	SIZE
LAWRENCE		
Beaver River, Little North Fork	Darlington, Rt. # 51	7.0 Miles
Deer Creek	Pulaski, Rt. # 208	2.5 Miles
Hickory Creek	Mt. Jackson, # 108	6.9 Miles
Neshannock Creek, Big	Volant, Rt. # 208	12.0 Miles
Bessemer Lake	Bessemer, Rt. # 317	28.0 Acres
Slippery Rock Creek	Harlansburg, Rt. # 19 & 108	9.0 Miles
Taylor Run	Harlansburg, Rt. # 19	3.4 Miles
MERCER		
Cool Spring Creek	Mercer, Rt. # 19	4.5 Miles
Deer Creek	Milledgeville, Rt. # 78	4.8 Miles
Mill Creek Trib. to Cool Spring Creek	Mercer, Rt. # 19	4.0 Miles
Mill Creek Trib. to French Creek	New Lebanon, Rt. # 78	4.5 Miles
Neshannock Creek	Mercer, Rt. # 19	8.0 Miles
Neshannock Creek, Little, West Branch	Hermitage, Rt. # 18	5.0 Miles
Pine Run	Mercer, Rt. # 19	3.5 Miles
Shenango River	Clark, Rt. # 18 & 258	1.0 Miles
Shenango River, Little	Hadley, off Rt. # 322	12.0 Miles
Wolf Creek, North Branch	Grove City, Rt. # 78	2.0 Miles
SOMERSET		
Allen Creek	New Lexington, Rt. # 53	2.3 Miles
Beaverdam Creek	Stoyestown, Rt. # 30	3.5 Miles
Beaverdam Run	Central City, Rt. # 160	5.0 Miles
Bens Creek	Ferndale, Rt. # 219	3.4 Miles
Bens Creek, South Fork	Ferndale, Rt. # 219	6.1 Miles
Blue Hole Run	New Lexington, Rt. # 53	1.4 Miles
Breastworks Run	New Baltimore, Rt. # 31	4.0 Miles
Brush Creek	Berlin, Rt. # 219	9.0 Miles
Casselman River	Boynton, Rt. # 219	5.9 Miles
Clear Run	Bakerville, Rt. # 31	2.5 Miles
Clear Shade Creek	Windber, Rt. # 56	8.0 Miles
Cub Run	Ogletown, Rt. # 56	2.0 Miles
Elklick Creek	Myersdale, Rt. # 219	3.6 Miles
Fall Creek	New Lexington, Rt. # 53	3.2 Miles
Flaugherty Creek	Myersdale, Rt. # 219	7.0 Miles
Gladdens Run	Hynman, Rt. # 96	1.0 Miles
Jones' Mill Run	Bakerville, Rt. # 31	3.9 Miles
Juniata River, Raystown Branch	New Baltimore, Rt. # 31	7.5 Miles
Kimberly Run	Somerset, Rt. # 219	2.5 Miles
Kooser Lake	Bakerville, Rt. # 31	4.0 Acres
Kooser Run	Friedens, Rt. # 53	3.0 Miles
Laurel Hill Creek	New Lexington, Rt. # 53	29.7 Miles
Laurel Lake	Trent, Rt. # 653	65.0 Acres
Laurel Run	Berlin, Rt. # 219	6.0 Miles
McClintock-Glade Runs	Fort Hill, Rt. # 53	4.6 Miles
Middle Creek	New Centerville, Rt. # 281	5.5 Miles
Miller Run	Meyersdale, Rt. # 219	3.0 Miles
Piney Creek, Big	Boynton, Rt. # 219	3.5 Miles
Piney Run	Central City, Rt. # 160	3.3 Miles
Piney Run, Little	Salisbury, Rt. # 219	2.7 Miles
Sandy Run	Sculton, Rt. # 653	2.0 Miles
Shafer Run	Bakerville, Rt. # 31	2.5 Miles
Shaffers Run	Fairhope, Rt. # 238	4.0 Miles

NAME OF WATER	MAP REFERENCE TOWN AND HIGHWAY	SIZE
Stony Creek	Shanksville, Off Rt. # 160	3.1 Miles
Tub Mill Run	Salisbury, Rt. # 219	2.0 Miles
White Creek	Confluence, Rt. # 53	9.1 Miles
Wills Creek	Berlin, Rt. # 219	16.0 Miles
Youghiogheny River	Confluence, Rt. # 53	1.0 Miles

VENANGO

Cherry Run	President, Rt. # 62	3.2 Miles
Horse Creek	Oil City, Rt. # 8	3.0 Miles
Mill Creek	Emlenton, Rt. # 208	4.4 Miles
Oil Creek	Rouseville, Rt. # 8	12.6 Miles
Pine Run	Jt. of Rt. # 322 & 38	5.0 Miles
Pithole Creek	Pleasantville, Rt. # 27	10.5 Miles
Porcupine Run	Cooperstown, Rt. # 427	1.0 Miles
Prather Creek	Cooperstown, Rt. # 427	3.0 Miles
Sandy Creek, Little	Polk, Rt. # 62	5.0 Miles
Sugar Creek	Sugar Creek, Rt. # 322	11.3 Miles
Sugar Creek, East Branch	Cooperstown, Rt. # 427	6.0 Miles
Sugar Creek, Little	Cooperstown, Rt. # 427	5.5 Miles
Two Mile Run, Lower	Franklin, Rt. # 8	3.5 Miles
Two Mile Run, Upper	Franklin, Rt. # 8	4.5 Miles
West Pithole Creek	Pleasantville, Rt. # 27	3.5 Miles
Scrubgrass Creek, Little	Lisbon, Rt. # 208	3.0 Miles
Hemlock Creek	President, Rt. # 62	1.0 Miles

WARREN

Ackley Run	Russell, Rt. # 62	5.0 Miles
Blue Eye Run	Garland, Rt. # 27	8.1 Miles
Brokenstraw Creek	Spring Creek, Rt. # 177	14.5 Miles
Brokenstraw Creek, Little	Pittsfield, Rt. # 6	9.1 Miles
Browns Run	Junction of Rt. # 6 & 59	7.0 Miles
Caldwell Creek	Grand Valley, Rt. # 27	4.0 Miles
Chapman Lake	Clarendon, Rt. # 6	68.0 Acres
Coffee Creek	Columbus, Rt. # 957	2.7 Miles
Farnsworth Branch	Clarendon, Rt. # 6	10.0 Miles
Four Mile Run	Saybrook, Rt. # 6	9.0 Miles
Hemlock Run	Glade, Rt. # 6	1.5 Miles
Hickory Creek, West	West Hickory, Rt. # 127	1.0 Miles
Jackson Run	Intersection of Rt. # 69 & 62	8.1 Miles
Perry McGee Run	Tidioute, Rt. # 127	5.0 Miles
Pine Creek	Enterprise, Rt. # 27	8.0 Miles
Reynolds Run	Russel, Rt. # 62	1.6 Miles
Rock Hollow Run	Tidioute, Rt. # 127	3.0 Miles
Six Mile Run	Tiona, Rt. # 6	5.0 Miles
Spring Creek	Spring Creek, Rt. # 77	4.0 Miles
Spring Creek, East Branch	Spring Creek, Rt. # 77	4.0 Miles
Thompson Run	Tidioute, Rt. # 127	2.0 Miles
Tidioute Creek	Tidioute, Rt. # 127	4.0 Miles
Tionesta Creek	Tionesta, Rt. # 62	5.0 Miles
Tionesta Creek, South Branch	Donaldson, Rt. # 948	11.0 Miles
Tionesta Creek, West Branch	Clarendon, Rt. # 6	12.0 Miles
Two Mile Run	Sheffield, Rt. # 6	14.0 Miles
Whitney Run (Spring Creek, Northwest Branch)	West Spring Creek, Rt. # 77	2.4 Miles

Summertime or wintertime, for the serious trout buff, there are plenty of productive waters.

NAME OF WATER	MAP REFERENCE TOWN AND HIGHWAY	SIZE
WASHINGTON		
Aunt Clara Fork	Florence, Rt. # 22	4.0 Miles
Bentleyville Municipal Authority Dam	Bentleyville, Rt. # 917	5.0 Acres
Canonsburg Lake	Donaldson's Crossroads, # 19	75.0 Acres
Dutch Fork Creek	Claysville, Rt. # 40	3.5 Miles
Dutch Fork Lake	Claysville, Rt. # 40	91.0 Acres
Enlow Fork	Majorsville	4.3 Miles
Kings Creek	Florence, Rt. # 22	3.0 Miles
Miller's Run	Intersection, Rt. # 50 & 978	4.5 Miles
Mingo Creek	Crookham, Rt. # 88	4.0 Miles
Pike Run	Daisytown, Rt. # 88	4.8 Miles
Templeton Fork	West Finley	2.5 Miles
Ten Mile Creek	Prosperity, Rt. # 18 & 221	3.0 Miles
WESTMORELAND		
Four Mile Run	Donegal, Rt. # 31	11.2 Miles
Hannas Run	Ligonier, Rt. # 30	1.6 Miles
Hendricks Run	West Fairfield, Rt. # 711	3.4 Miles
Indian Creek	Champion, Rt. # 711	2.0 Miles
Jacobs Creek	Laurelville, Rt. # 982	3.0 Miles
Keystone Lake	New Alexandria, Rt. # 22	78.0 Acres
Linn Run	Rector, Rt. # 381	2.0 Miles
Loyalhanna Creek	Ligonier, Rt. # 30	10.0 Miles
Mill Creek	Waterford, Rt. # 711	6.5 Miles
Roaring Run	Jones Mills, Rt. # 31	3.5 Miles
Shannon Run	New Florence, Rt. # 711	3.0 Miles
Sewickley Creek, Lt.	Arona, Rt. # 136	3.2 Miles
Tub Mill Run	New Florence, Rt. # 711	5.7 Miles
Twin Lake, Lower	Crabtree, Rt. # 119	30.0 Acres

FISHERMAN'S FAVORITES THE TOP 100 PLUS STREAMS

With such an abundance of trout waters available in Pennsylvania it is inevitable that certain streams will emerge as favorites with the fishermen. Favorites generally gain their status because they generally produce a steady volume of trout, are usually accessible to plenty of fishermen and maintain a favorable and consistent level of water. For the most part the favorites we are listing are your best bet for either fly fishing or bait fishing.

A consensus of trout anglers and the Pennsylvania Fish Commission agree that the following streams, representing a variety of sizes and conditions, fall into the category of "fishin' favorites," and we invite you to try for yourself and perhaps add them to your favorite list.

All streams mentioned are open to either bait fishing or fly fishing, and can easily be located by the map references. Simply take an ordinary highway map, and pinpoint the streams by the Route Number, Town and County, all of which are shown for each body of water. We should mention that since Pennsylvania stocks trout in a large number of lakes and ponds, we have included them as well, with the acreage shown. Streams are shown in fishable miles.

An excellent source of current trout information can be gained by visiting the sporting goods stores in the area you plan to fish. Local citizens can be very helpful in passing on information regarding current hatches, feeding times and productive areas. Some that we have patronized are listed elsewhere in this guide, and we suggest that you take a few minutes to visit them when you are in the area.

STREAMS & COUNTY

ADAMS COUNTY

CONEWAGO CREEK — Best trout fishing water in the county. Rt. 234, the scenic valley route, parallels a section of the stream known as "The Narrows." There is natural reproduction of brown trout within this section of stream.

BEDFORD COUNTY

JUNIATA RIVER, RAYSTOWN BRANCH — A 10 mile stretch. Reached at Manns Choice, Rt. 31 and Bedford, Rt. 30.

YELLOW CREEK — 18 miles, at Loysburg, Rt. 36.

BERKS COUNTY

SCOTTS RUN LAKE — 21 acre lake in French Creek State Park. Good winter trout fishing.

BLAIR COUNTY

CANOE LAKE — Located at village of Canoe Creek, Rt. 22. Excellent ice-fishing. Electric motors and rowboats.

CLOVER CREEK — 17.5 miles. At Rt. 164 from Martinsburg to reach the upper end of the stream. Williamsburg on the lower stretch. Classic meadow fishing for brown trout. Reproduction of brown trout in some areas.

PINEY CREEK — 6.5 miles. Rt. 866 at Royer (Fish Commission access). Reproduction of brown trout.

BRADFORD COUNTY

SCHRADER CREEK — Can be reached at Powell, off Rt. 414, or Leroy on Rt. 414 via Sunfish Pond.

BUCKS COUNTY

COOKS CREEK — Flowing through gently rolling farm country, this stream is located in Northern Bucks County along Rt. 212 and 412 near Springtown.

BUTLER COUNTY

BUFFALO CREEK — 10 miles east of Butler. Take LR 10036 north from Rt. 422, through Fenelton to T570 to the Hicky Bottom area. Fish early season with live bait.

CAMERON COUNTY

CLEAR CREEK — Five miles north of Emporium, off Rt. 46.

DRIFTWOOD BRANCH — Stretch running parallel to Rt. 120, Driftwood to Emporium.

SINNEMAHONING CREEK, FIRST FORK — Runs parallel to Rt. 872.

GEORGE B. STEVENSON DAM — Located on Rt. 872 at Lushbaugh. 142 acre lake, electric motors allowed.

CARBON COUNTY

LEHIGH RIVER — Off Rt. 940 or I-80. 10 mile stretch from Francis E. Walter Dam, downstream past White Haven to mouth of Sandy Run, fairly accessible. Wilderness area between mouth of Tobyhanna Creek to head of the Walters impoundment.

CENTRE COUNTY

BALD EAGLE CREEK — Parallels Rt. 220. Best fishing from Unionville to Milesburg in early part of season.

ELK CREEK — From Smulltown to Coburn and junction with Penns Creek. Millheim is middle to Elk Creek fishing.

PENNS CREEK — From Spring Mills to Coburn, good road parallels entire length of stream.

SPRING CREEK — Fisherman's Paradise. Six-tenths of a mile from lower boundary of Spring Creek. Hatchery grounds to the upper boundary of the Paradise. Special regulations apply.

CHESTER COUNTY

FRENCH CREEK — Best water area in the county, stocked from St. Peters to Phoenixville. Reached easily from Rt. 23, paralleling the stream frequently.

CLARION COUNTY

CANOE CREEK — East of Knox and Wentling Corners. Rt. 338 and LR 16033.

LEATHERWOOD CREEK — Along Rt. 854 at Rockville.

BROOK TROUT (Salvelinus fontinalis)

CLEARFIELD COUNTY

CHEST CREEK — Rt. 36 from Mahaffey to Westover.

MOSQUITO CREEK — Rt. 879 out of Clearfield to Frenchville. Difficult access, but a peaceful setting and good fishing reward the willing angler.

TROUT DAM — Take Rt. 879 out of Clearfield. Trout Run empties into West Branch of the Susquehanna River at Shawville.

CLINTON COUNTY

FISHING CREEK — Off Rt. 220 at Mill Hall.

YOUNG WOMAN'S CREEK, RIGHT BRANCH — Fly-Fishing-Only area, 6 miles, from confluence with the Left Branch up to Beechwood Trail.

COLUMBIA COUNTY

FISHING CREEK — From Orangeville, Rt. 330 upstream to Grassmere Park.

CRAWFORD COUNTY

CONNEAUT CREEK — Rt. 198 intersects the stream west of Conneautville. Good fishing up or downstream.

OIL CREEK — Centerville on Rt. 8 downstream to Hydetown.

WOODCOCK CREEK — The stream parallels Rt. 198 east of Saegertown before crossing just west of Blooming Valley.

CUMBERLAND COUNTY

OPOSSUM LAKE — 60 acre lake five miles west of Carlisle. Take Rt. 641. Electric motors permitted.

YELLOW BREECHES CREEK — 38 miles of limestone water. Headwaters can be reached by Rt. 233 at Huntsdale. For other points on the stream, take Rt. 34 from Carlisle, Rt. 15 from Dillsburg and Rt. 74 from Carlisle.

BIG SPRING CREEK — A picturesque limestone stream flowing five miles through the heart of the beautiful Cumberland Valley. The stream abounds with native Brook Trout. Fish-For-Fun area is located near the headwaters. Take Rt. 233 going upstream from Newville.

DAUPHIN COUNTY

CLARKS CREEK — Follow Rt. 322 to Rt. 225 at Dauphin; take Rt. 225 until it intersects with 325. Stream parallels Rt. 325 for 22 miles. Rt. 209 also intersects Rt. 325 coming from the north.

DELAWARE COUNTY

RIDLEY CREEK — In Ridley Creek State Park. Area is heavily wooded, the stream clean and clear. Seven miles of water in the park. Fly-Fishing-Only area extends from the falls downstream to the mouth of Dismal Run.

ELK COUNTY

BEAR CREEK — In Allegheny National Forest. Reached from Ridgway on Forest Service Road 135 to FSR 134 for upper half of stream. FSR 20 out of Ridgway for lower half. Camping area, no charge.

CLARION RIVER, WEST BRANCH — Along Rt. 219. 10 mile stretch Johnsonburg to Elk-McKean County line famous for big brown trout. Excellent minnow and worm fishing in late April and early May. Fly fishing excellent late May through summer months.

RIDGWAY RESERVOIR — 75 acres. One mile from Ridgway. Especially good trout fishing during winter trout season. No boats.

SPRING CREEK — In Allegheny National Forest. A large, fast moving stream with lots of rock pockets. Excellent wet fly fishing. Located at Hallton and upstream along Forest Service Roads 20 and 130.

WILSON RUN — Along Rt. 321 between Kane and Wilcox. Six mile stretch runs through meadows and wooded areas.

MEDIX RUN — Located at village of Medix Run on Rt. 555. Seven mile stretch of stream, beginning in Clearfield County runs crystal clear and cold.

ERIE COUNTY

FRENCH CREEK, SOUTH BRANCH — Located in the southwest corner of the county at Corry. Take Rt. 6 south. Stocked from Corry to Elgin.

LITTLE CONNEAUTTEE CREEK — Off Rt. 6, three miles north of Edinboro.

BROWN TROUT (Salmo trutta)

FOREST COUNTY

EAST HICKORY CREEK — East of Endeavor on Rt. 666. Good fishing throughout the season.

SALMON CREEK — West of Marienville. Take Forest Service Road 22 or LR 27010 to FSR 145.

SPRING CREEK — Off Rt. 66 at Pigeon on FSR 131. Stream can also be reached along T327 near Duhring.

TIONESTA CREEK — Along Rt. 666 from Kellettville to Warren County line.

WARDS RANCH POND — Located off Rt. 66 at Vowinckel on T344.

FRANKLIN COUNTY

FALLING SPRING BRANCH — Outstanding limestone stream. Fly-Fishing-Only area extends for one mile from property line of Leonard Zeger and Valley Quarries to Robert Gabler Farm near I-80. Fish-For-Fun area begins at LR 28003 in Aqua, extends downstream 0.75 mile

LETTERKENNY RESERVOIR — Roxbury, Rt. 641. 54 acres, electric motors permitted. Boat mooring area. Excellent winter trout fishing; ice fishing permitted.

JEFFERSON COUNTY

RED BANK CREEK — Flows south from Brookville. Contains many stretches of beautiful water, and is accessible by Rt. 28. This stream offers a float trip of ease for the canoeist, with unlimited remote beauty.

RED BANK CREEK, NORTH FORK — Flow south to Brookville from the Elk-Jefferson County line. Crystalline, natural and wild, you have to walk to enjoy the fine angling on this stream. Rt. 968 follows the valley of the North Fork north from Brookville to Munderf.

LACKAWANNA COUNTY

LEHIGH RIVER — Rt. 611, Clifton-Thornhurst Road takes you to the stream. Best area is water adjacent to SGL #135 at Plank Road Bridge, downstream to the confluence of the Lehigh and Ash Creek.

LANCASTER COUNTY

OCTORARO CREEK, WEST BRANCH — Pennsylvania Dutch country, with fine trout fishing in the southern part of the country. Fly-Fishing-Only area included on this stream beginning near Rt. 141, extending downstream to T334.

LAWRENCE COUNTY

BIG NESHANNOCK CREEK — This stream offers good fishing to Western Pennsylvania anglers. It can be reached at Volant, Rt. 278.

SLIPPERY ROCK CREEK — Features a half mile stretch of Fish-For-Fun water extending 0.25 mile on either side of the Armstrong Bridge on LR 37052. Plenty of "open trout fishing water, too." Follow Rt. 422.

LEBANON COUNTY

CONEWAGO CREEK — From Lawn upstream along Rt. 241 and Rt. 117 to Mt. Gretna.

HAMMER CREEK — Reached over Rt. 322. Best fishing from Buffalo Springs, downstream.

LIONS LAKE — Also called Lights Dam. 20 acres. Take Rt. 72 North of Lebanon to Ebenezer.

MARQUETTE LAKE — 15 acre lake. Artificial lures only. Rt. 443 north from Indiantown Gap Military Reservation.

LEHIGH COUNTY

LITTLE LEHIGH CREEK — Flows through the city of Allentown. 12 mile stretch is stocked beginning near the confluence with the Lehigh River upstream to Brookdale off Rt. 100. Stream meanders through open farmlands until it reaches Allentown where it runs through the city's park system.

LUZERNE COUNTY

HARVEY CREEK — This stream offers good fishing and is accessible at several areas as Rt. 29 closely follows the stream, crossing at several points. Begin at West Nanticoke.

HARVEYS LAKE — 658 acre natural lake offers excellent winter trout fishing. One of only several Pennsylvania lakes holding lake trout.

LYCOMING COUNTY

LITTLE PINE CREEK — Take Rt. 44 north from the town of Waterville.

LOYALSOCK CREEK — Rt. 87 parallels the stream from the town of Montoursville. Includes a 3 mile Fly-Fishing-Only area from Lycoming County line downstream.

PINE CREEK — Rts. 44 and 414 follow this stream north from Waterville. Rt. 414 closely follows the creek through Jersey Mills to Cammal.

SLATE RUN — Take Rt. 414 to the village of Slate Run. Stream parallels forestry road. 6.5 mile stretch in Brown Township in Fly-Fishing-Only water.

McKEAN COUNTY

KINZUA CREEK, SOUTH BRANCH — Located about four miles north of Kane along Rt. 321.

MARVIN CREEK — Can be reached by taking Rt. 6. Located between Hazelhurst and Smethport.

POTATO CREEK — Along Rt. 46 between Smethport and Betula.

TIONESTA CREEK, EAST BRANCH — Located along Forest Service Road 133 between Jo Jo and Ludlow.

MERCER COUNTY

DEER CREEK — Located just south of the Crawford County line on Rt. 173, three miles east of Rt. 79. Very good fishing, but not fished hard due to its location.

LITTLE SHENANGO RIVER — About 14 miles stocked by the Fish Commission. Located just off Rt. 358, running east and west out of Greenville.

NESHANNOCK CREEK — 18 miles of trout water. Easily reached at several points off Rt. 19. Fish-For-Fun area stretches for one mile between Rt. 258 and Rt. 58.

SHENANGO RIVER — Stocked with trout for about one mile below the dam outlet. Near Sharpsville.

MONROE COUNTY

BIG BUSHKILL CREEK — Can be reached via Rt. 209 at Bushkill or Rt. 402 near Resica Falls Scout Reservation. Fly-Fishing-Only area extends for six miles on the Reservation, excluding a 400 yard stretch on either side of the falls.

MONTGOMERY COUNTY

SKIPPACK CREEK — Eight miles of trout water within Evansburg State Park. Extends from Evansburg State Park Bridge to Forty Foot Road.

UNAMI CREEK — Heavily fished, this two mile stretch of good trout water is located near Sumneytown. Use Rt. 63 or Sumneytown Pike. Area runs from Camp Delmont Scout Camp to and including Camp University.

NORTHAMPTON COUNTY

BUSHKILL CREEK — From Tatamy to Thirteenth Street in Easton. Bushkill Drive parallels the stream.

MONOCACY CREEK — Beginning at National Portland Cement Company, extending downstream to Brodheads at Rt. 22. Rt. 191 crosses the stream at Hecktown.

PERRY COUNTY

LAUREL RUN — Flowing through a wilderness area in the Tuscarora State Forest, this stream offers native brook trout its entire 13½ mile length. In addition, it is stocked from Phoenix Mills to Sherman Creek. The stream is located southwest of Landisburg. Take Rt. 233 to a fork in the road; bear right past Laurel Inn.

PHILADELPHIA COUNTY

WISSAHICKON CREEK — Flowing through Fairmount Park, the Wissahickon offers the only trout fishing in the Commonwealth's largest metropolitan area. Take Ridge Avenue, Germantown Avenue, Rt. 422 or Henry Avenue. Parking areas are adjacent to the stream; driving is prohibited on the bridle paths.

PIKE COUNTY

LACKAWAXEN RIVER — Can be reached by taking LR 51018 from Rt. 590 east of Hawley to Kimbles, or Rt. 434 off Rt. 6 to Rt. 590, then west on Rt. 590 to the stream.

SHOHOLA CREEK — Rt. 6 to Shohola Falls, or Rt. 739 to the head of Shohola Falls Dam. I-84 runs parallel to the stream. This section is float-stocked.

WALLENPAUPACK CREEK — Reached by taking Rt. 507 to Newfoundland or Greentown.

POTTER COUNTY

ALLEGHENY RIVER — From Potter-McKean County line to Seven Bridges. Take Rt. 6 and 49.

KETTLE CREEK — From the Potter-Clinton County line to Oleona. Take Rt. 144.

LYMAN RUN DAM — Located 12 miles east of Coudersport, south of Rt. 6.

OSWAYO CREEK — Sharon Center to Oswayo, Rt. 44.

PINE CREEK — Potter-Tioga County line to Brookland, Rt. 6.

PINE CREEK, WEST BRANCH — Galeton to Corbett, Rt. 6.

SINNEMAHONING CREEK, EAST FORK — Wharton to Conrad, Rt. 872 at Wharton.

SINNEMAHONING CREEK, FIRST FORK — Potter-Cameron County line to Costello, Rt. 872.

SCHUYLKILL COUNTY

DEEP CREEK — 10 miles of stream located in Hegins Valley on Rt. 125.

LIZZARD CREEK — Five miles of good trout water along Rt. 309. Stream flows into Andreas.

MAHANTANGO CREEK — Located in Mahantango Valley on LR 53047. East of Klingerstown. Six miles of water.

SOMERSET COUNTY

LAUREL HILL CREEK — 29 miles of stream. Reached at Bakersville, Rt. 31 and Confluence, Rt. 281.

WHITES CREEK — 4.5 miles of water reached at Confluence off Rt. 281.

WILLS CREEK — Located at Berlin on Rt. 160 or Fairhope, Rt. 288.

YOUGHIOGHENY RIVER — A three mile stretch reached at Confluence off Rt. 281. Open for year around trout fishing in the tailrace below the Youghiogheny Dam.

RAINBOW TROUT (Salmo gairdnerii)

SULLIVAN COUNTY

LITTLE LOYALSOCK CREEK — Rt. 87 parallels the stream from Forksville to Cherry Mills.

SUSQUEHANNA COUNTY

SNAKE CREEK — This stream parallels Rt. 29 north of Montrose.

STARRUCCA CREEK — Take Rt. 81 to Hallstead, then go east on Rt. 171 to the vicinity of Lanesboro.

QUAKER LAKE — Follow Rt. 106 to Montrose, then north on Rt. 29 to Lawsville Center. Pick up LR 57075 going west a distance of six miles.

TIOGA COUNTY

PINE CREEK — Flows through the famous Pennsylvania Grand Canyon. Can be reached from Rt. 6 between Ansonia and Galeton and at Tiadaghton State Park. Also along Rt. 414 at Blackwell.

UNION COUNTY

PENNS CREEK — Located in Union and Centre Counties, best fishing area is from Glen Iron upstream into Centre County. Take Rt. 235 south from Laurelton to Glen Iron. Big Drake or Shad Fly late May to early June.

This stream attracts some canoe traffic during the early part of the season, and the best fishing, and least canoes, will be in early summer when the waters recede.

VENANGO COUNTY

OIL CREEK, TRIBUTARY TO ALLEGHENY RIVER — Rt. 8 crosses the stream north of Rouseville. Also follow LR 60045 north.

WARREN COUNTY

ALLEGHENY RESERVOIR — Excellent ice fishing in and around the Kinzua Arm.

BROKENSTRAW CREEK — Between Youngsville and Spring Creek, along Rt. 6 and Rt. 77.

CHAPMAN DAM — Best times during April, May and early June throughout the lake, and in the upper portions in mid and late summer. Excellent winter ice fishing.

KINZUA DAM TAILWATERS — Extends one mile downstream from the dam. Year around trout fishing, limit three trout per day.

LITTLE BROKENSTRAW CREEK — Located between Pittsfield and Lottsville, along Rt. 6 and Rt. 958.

WARREN COUNTY, (Continued)

PINE CREEK — Best fishing east of Grand Valley in area known as Seldom Seen, downstream to East Titusville. Take LR 61001.

TIONESTA CREEK — Downstream from Barnes to the Forest County line along Rt. 666.

WAYNE COUNTY

BIG DYBERRY CREEK — Best waters are north of the Jadwin Dry Dam. Take Rt. 191 north of Honesdale three miles and turn left ½ mile. Good fly fishing waters.

WYOMING COUNTY

BOWMAN'S CREEK — Good waters from Noxen to Eatonville. Follow Rt. 29 and Rt. 309.

MEHOOPANY CREEK — Rt. 87 to Forkston parallels the stream on the east; LR 65051 on the west.

YORK COUNTY

MUDDY CREEK — Best waters a 2½ mile stretch from Woodbine to Castle Fin. Take Rt. 74 south from York to Airville. From Airville follow Rt. 425 south to Woodbine. Castle Fin is about two miles downstream.

Numerous lakes and ponds receive generous stockings of trout and offer excellent fishing to the angler who prefers fishing large bodies of water.

Another scoop of lively trout destined for release in Pennsylvania public waters.

NORTHWEST REGION — 1281 Otter St., Box 349, Franklin, Pa. 16323
Ph. 814-437-5774

Counties: Butler, Clarion, Crawford, Erie, Forest, Jefferson, Lawrence, McKean, Mercer, Venango, Warren.

SOUTHWEST REGION — R.D. #2, Box 39, Somerset, Pa. 15501
Ph. 814-445-8974

Counties: Allegheny, Armstrong, Beaver, Cambria, Fayette, Greene, Indiana, Somerset, Washington, Westmoreland.

NORTH CENTRAL REGION — Box 688, Lock Haven, Pa. 17745
Ph. 717-748-5396

Counties: Cameron, Centre, Clearfield, Clinton, Elk, Lycoming, Potter, Snyder, Sullivan, Tioga, Union.

SOUTH CENTRAL REGION — R.D. #3, Box 109, Mifflintown, Pa. 17059
Ph. 717-436-2117

Counties: Adams, Bedford, Blair, Cumberland, Franklin, Fulton, Huntingdon, Juniata, Mifflin, Perry, York.

NORTHEAST REGION — Box 88, Sweet Valley, Pa. 18656
Ph. 717-477-5717

Counties: Bradford, Carbon, Columbia, Lackawanna, Luzerne, Monroe, Montour, Northumberland, Pike, Susquehanna, Wayne, Wyoming.

SOUTHEAST REGION — Box 6, Elm, Pa. 17521
Ph. 717-626-0228

Counties: Berks, Bucks, Chester, Dauphin, Delaware, Lancaster, Lebanon, Lehigh, Montgomery, Northampton, Philadelphia, Schuylkill.

A youngster has his first encounter with a nice trout. I am sure we can relate our early days to this scene.

McClure
Hale Eddy
Cadosia
Winterdale
Hancock
Fishs Eddy
East Branch Delaware
French Woods
Stevens Point
Brandt
Melrose
Scott Center
Starlight
Starrucca
Shehawken
Stockport
Preston Park
Preston Center
Lordville
Long Eddy
Thompson
Lake Como
Equinunk
Lakewood
Stalker
Orson
Poyntelle
Priceville
Braman
Hankins
East Ararat
Rock Lake
Lookout
Duck Harbor Pond
Callicoon
Pleasant Mount
Herrick Center
Niagara
Cold Spring
Galilee
Union Dale
Whites Valley
Rileyville
West Damascus
Damascus
Cochecton
WAYNE
Stillwater Dam
Forest City
Creamton
Siko
Girdland
Milanville
Aldenville
Boyds Mills
Vandling
Dyberry
PROMPTON
Atco
Bethany
Gen Edgar Jadwin Res
Prompton Lake
Laurella
Beach Lake
Narrowsburg
Simpson
Prompton
Waymart
Honesdale
STATE HOSP
Carbondale
Indian Orchard
Mayfield
Jermyn
Masthope
ARCHBALD POTHOLE
Hoadleys
South Canaan
White Mills
Archbald
Bohemia
Varden
Gravity
Lake Paupackan
Hawley
Cortez
Lake Ariel
Uswick
Kimbles
Delaware River
Equinunk Creek
Lackawanna
10
17
30
70
97
106
159
170
171
191
236
247
296
370
371
590
652
670
6

TROUT FISHING ON THE UPPER DELAWARE RIVER

One stretch of fine trout water generally overlooked, or unknown, by many Pennsylvania fishermen is the upper portion of the Delaware River. Good trout waters begin at the vicinity of Callicoon, N.Y., and extend upstream to the town of Hancock, N.Y., thence the west branch to a point just below Hale Eddy, N.Y. This section of water contains an abundance of brown and rainbow trout, many ranging in the five pound class. The small legion of anglers who fish this section on a regular basis classify the Upper Delaware as the best in the East, and recent articles appearing in national publications have substantiated their claim. As far as rainbows are concerned, it has few if any equals. Ironically, many notable anglers have never fished its waters.

The Upper Delaware River received controlled cool water releases from the New York City reservoirs at Cannonsville and Pepacton, which commence about the first of June and continue into the fall. The releases stabilize the temperature at about 72 degrees and has resulted in a large number of wild rainbow and brown being naturally hatched. No hatchery fish are released, but there is no need. The river has attained a point of abundance in both species that will grow to trophy sizes. However, they are very intelligent and are a challenge to any angler.

Fishing between Callicoon and the West Branch is very good, and there are countless numbers of rapids, long pools and rocky areas to satisfy the preference of any fisherman. The best trout fishing generally starts about the end of May and is excellent throughout the summer and early fall. During the early months of May and June, any method is productive. If you are a live bait fisherman nightcrawlers and minnows are the best. For the spin fisherman, just about any flashing lure is good, with the brown showing some preference for gold ones, while the rainbows seem to be most attracted to silver. For the live bait or spin caster use at least a six-pound test line and a size six or eight hook.

Father and daughter maneuver for a favorable position in the swift water.

The Upper Delaware River is a fly fisherman's delight since it offers many long stretches of productive waters and generally uncrowded conditions. Although you have a special preference in flies, to start with we suggest using either dark or light Cahills or Stoneflys. One point to keep in mind is that larger artificials and hooksizes are a must. The trout will run above average in size and are very active fighters. Coupled with the water current, you will have better results with the larger lures. Use either a size six or eight hook, long shank, and if you are tying your own flies, be sure to make sure to prepare some specials for the Delaware. For streamers, we suggest a size six and for nymphs, a size eight.

There is one annoying problem to contend with, the river is subjected to heavy canoe traffic, especially on weekends. However, most of the canoes are launched nearer to Callicoon, thus if you are planning to fish a weekend, we suggest that you try the upper reaches. During the week, there are few canoes and any area can be fished with few interferences.

The Upper Delaware River can easily be reached by following Route 191 to Hancock, N.Y. From that point there is a paved road that follows the stream towards Hale Eddy. Route 191 also parallels the river down stream for several miles. The river can also be reached via paved roads to Lordville, Stalker and Callicoon. There are some additional paved secondary roads from these points, offering some fine access points. There is considerable private property, however permission is usually granted if you ask.

One good method of fishing is via a float trip. If you possess a suitable Jon boat or canoe, you should consider floating and fishing. This method will give you the opportunity to fish more waters, plus many unreachable from most access areas. Boats must be launched from designated ramp sites, and free launches are operated by the Pennsylvania Fish Commission at BALLS EDDY on the West Branch just north of Hancock, at BUCKINGHAM, just North of Equinuck off Route 191, and on the Pennsylvania side of CALLICOON, just a short distance below the bridge.

This variety of flies that will produce trout on the Upper Delaware River. Note the sizes in relation to the ruler.

85

Plenty of quality water and a natural trout hatchery produces fine fishing and trophy sized trout on the Upper Delaware River.

    A final note, be sure to check your compendium of regulations, since special rules apply to the Upper Delaware River.

    An excellent source of current information is the D&K Sport Shop at Callicoon, N.Y. The owner, Don Meckle, fishes the Delaware extensively and will be glad to supply up-to-the minute data on stream conditions, lures, and hatch activity. In addition, D&K carries a full line of Delaware River flies plus all other fishing and hunting equipment. The shop opens daily at 9:00 A.M., and is located just one block from the Callicoon Bridge on the New York side. If you wish to call ahead the number is 914-887-4857.

ANGLER RECOGNITION PROGRAM

With the possibility always present that you may catch and successfully land a trophy sized trout, be sure not to overlook the ANGLER RECOGNITION PROGRAM, which is open to all licensed anglers, both adult and juniors under sixteen years of age. The purpose of the program is to recognize and issue awards of excellence to any angler taking a large trout that meets the minimum size requirements.

No special fee is involved, but you must follow the specific rules listed in this article, which also gives the minimum size requirements. For those lucky anglers who qualify for an award, the Fish Commission will present a beautiful angler's certificate, plus an embroidered emblem to attach to your favorite jacket or shirt. Your emblem will serve notice to all that your big one did not get away.

To receive a copy of the official entry form, write to the Pennsylvania Fish Commission, Anglers Award Office, Box 1673, Harrisburg, Penna. 17020. Oh yes, be sure to have your camera handy since a photo of your catch will be required.

Rules for Anglers Award

1. Fish must be caught in Pennsylvania waters that are open to the public without charge or fee. Fish taken in farm ponds, fee fishing lakes, ponds or streams, or in waters restricted to use by club members or their guests do not qualify.

2. Fish must be caught in its legally open season by legal methods.

3. Fish must be measured and weighed by any License Issuing Agent or tackle store or an employee of the Pennsylvania Fish Commission.

4. Measurement of length and girth must be made with the use of a metal ruler or tape.

5. Good, clear photos of the fish should accompany the Angler Award application but are not required if the fish has been certified by an Official Measuring Station or Fish Commission employee. (State Record application **does** require a photo.)

6. The Angler Awards Program is open to both residents and non-residents.

7. Persons under 16 years of age are eligible for a Junior Award (see minimum sizes) but in all cases, only one patch will be issued. Anglers may submit as many fish of a single species meeting minimum requirements as they may catch, but only one patch will be awarded annually.

8. To be considered as a STATE RECORD, the fish must be weighed on a certified scale and witnessed by one person, not including the angler and any companions accompanying him or her at the time of catch. Also, separate Application for State Record must be completed.

9. Applications for Angler Awards or State Records must be received within 30 days of the catch in order to qualify.

MINIMUM SIZES FOR AWARD CONSIDERATION

	Adults Inches	Juniors Inches	State Record Inches
Trout, rainbow, palomino	24	20	27½
Trout, brown	24	20	34
Trout, brook	17	14	25⅜
Salmon, Coho	28	26	31½
Salmon, Steelhead	30	28	40¼

How to measure your fish, and be sure to include a clear photo.

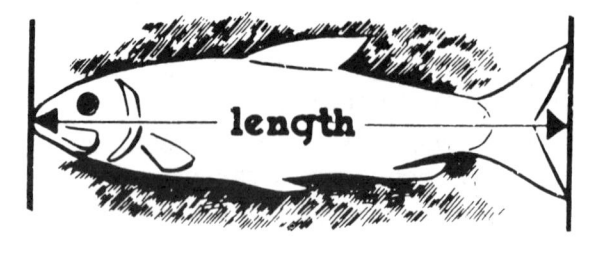

ERIE COUNTY SALMON COHO—CHINOOK

A delightful bonus to Pennsylvania sportsmen who fish the western portion of the state is the annual return of the Coho and Chinook Salmon into the tributary waters of Erie County. These fish represent an exciting addition to the waters of Lake Erie as well as the tributaries, and each fall more fishermen are joining the thousands who journey to Erie County for this fall event. The lure of landing one of these super poundage fighters is difficult to resist.

Taking a cue from the successful program of Michigan, in 1969 the Pennsylvania Fish Commission initiated a continuing project of planting Coho and Chinook fry in the tributary waters, which has proven to be a tremendous success. Schedules call for the annual release of Coho fry in the spring, and although some Chinooks are released at the same time, the bulk of the Chinooks are held for release after September.

The eggs are hatched and youngsters reared by the state hatchers at nearby Fairview, Penna., and when ready for release they will measure from 4-6 inches in length. Once placed in the streams they will commence their downstream trek into Lake Erie to mature. About eighteen months later, the Coho will start to appear as adults and will have attained a size averaging thirty inches in length and about eight pounds in weight. The Chinooks remain in the lake for an extended period of from three to five years before they return. They will tip the scales at about fifteen to seventeen pounds and be from thirty to thirty-six inches long. Like their Pacific relative, once the spawning ritual is completed, their life cycle has ended. Those that are not taken by fishermen will perish.

As early as July both fish will begin to gather off shore in anticipation of the fall run, and will remain there until cooler temperatures and fall rains arrive. During this interim, they will congregate in large schools, and fishermen with suitable boats equipped with downriggers can take them by trolling various spoons. The fish can be found from one to eight miles from the shore line. If you do have a boat with the proper equipment, the Pennsylvania Fish Commission operates and maintains a free launch area at Walnut Creek entry. We suggest that you call ahead for conditions and traffic at the launch. The launch can be reached by calling 814-833-2464, and is open daily.

September finds many large Coho salmon entering Pennsylvania streams. When they do, many anglers will await them.

As the cooler days of September arrive, the Coho and Chinooks will begin moving into streams, where they will be greeted by many anglers. Similar to the American Shad that migrates up the Delaware River, the Coho and Chinook do not feed during their run, and will only strike at artificial lures. They can be taken on a variety of spinners, bucktails and streamers. The recommended hook size is a number three, using at least a fifteen pound test line and steel leader. As far as colors are concerned, the fish will strike indiscriminately, although many of the more successful fishermen claim that black or other similar dark colors produce the best results. Check what is producing and be governed accordingly.

During the run, there is excellent fishing from the Lake Erie shore line near the tributaries, and the line of anglers closely resembles saltwater fishing on the east coast. Anglers outfitted with chest high waders can comfortably wade far enough to be within casting distance of the fish. At this time of the year the water is normally moderate to calm.

A fine Coho, typical of those that invade waters of Erie County each fall.

scattered small spots

no spots

black mouth with white gums

long and shallow

COHO SALMON

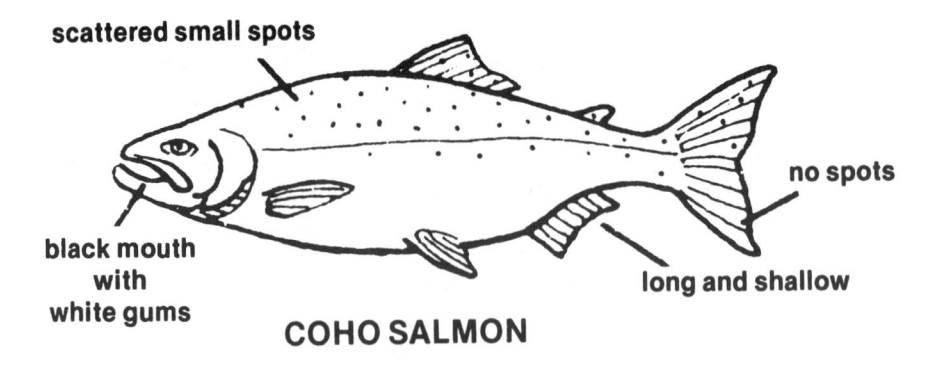

(spawning condition: reddish with enlarged jaw)

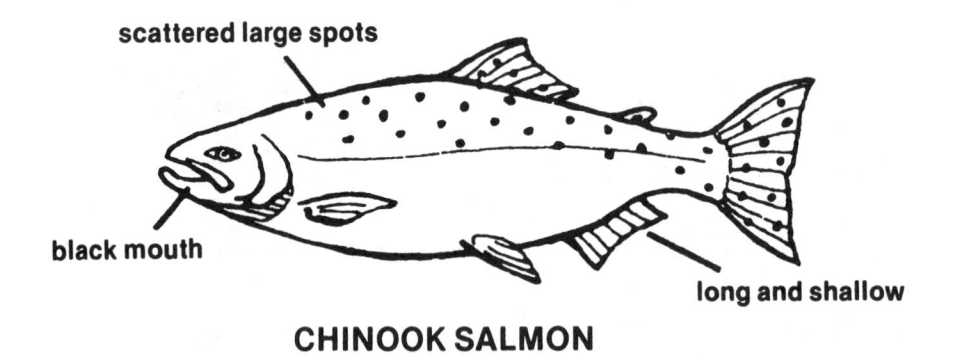

---

scattered large spots

black mouth

long and shallow

CHINOOK SALMON

(spawning condition: dark coloring and enlarged jaw)

Fishing in the tributaries becomes understandably crowded, and we suggest that you plan your trip carefully to maximize your fishing time. Coho fishing remains good from September right up to the arrival of cold weather. On the other hand, the Chinook will generally terminate their run by the end of October. In the streams, good results can be achieved after periods of moderate rain. The streams are accessible and clearly marked for entry. Please check our map

SUCCESSFUL TROLLING RIGS

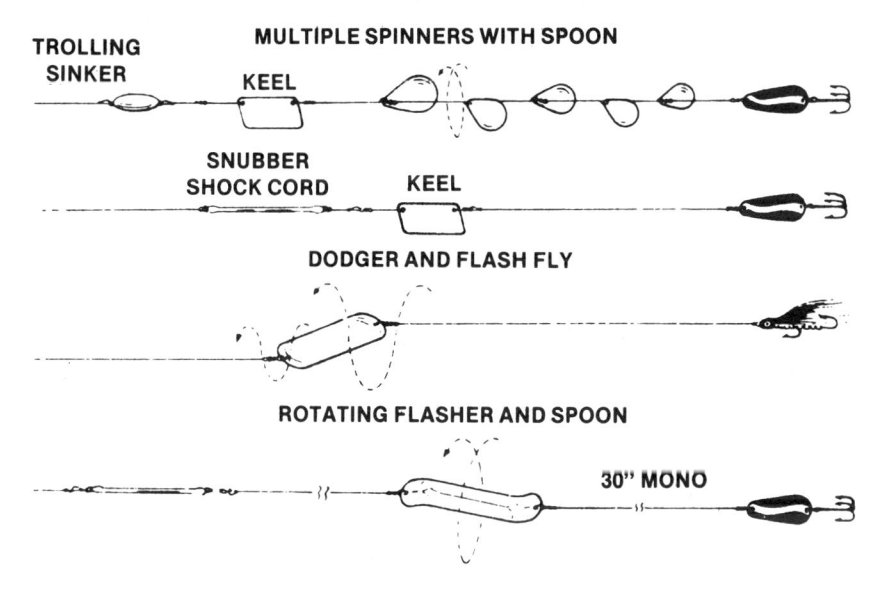

MULTIPLE SPINNERS WITH SPOON

TROLLING SINKER — KEEL

SNUBBER SHOCK CORD — **KEEL**

DODGER AND FLASH FLY

ROTATING FLASHER AND SPOON

30" MONO

for a general location of the streams, and when in the area, check the local sports shops for prevailing conditions and best locations to fish. The daily limit is six, any combination of Coho or Chinook, no minimum size.

Be sure to observe posted regulations where applicable, and always respect the private lands where posted, and always be a good sportsman. Do not litter and be considerate of your fellow angler. Also bear in mind, unlike other states that permit the practice, ALL COHO and CHINOOK MUST BE TAKEN BY HOOK AND LINE ONLY, POSITIVELY NO SNAGGING OR FOULHOOKING IS PERMITTED.

If you are planning to visit Erie County this fall, we suggest that you take a moment and write to the Erie County Tourist Bureau, 1006 State St., Erie, Penna. 16501. Ask for a packet detailing services and accommodations available to the fishermen who are planning to stay for a few days. If you are looking for daily fishing information, there is an Erie fishing Hotline that will give you accurate up-to-the-minute reports on salmon fishing. The number is 814-833-2377 and is in operation from June 1 to the end of October.

PUBLIC LAUNCH AREAS

CITY OF ERIE, PA., Chestnut St., two blocks west of State St. NO FEE, six commercial marinas located east and west of the Erie Public Dock.

PRESQUE ISLE STATE PARK, Total of seven ramps

WALNUT CREEK ACCESS, Maintained by the Fish Commission, four miles west of Erie at the mouth of Walnut Creek. Open daily 5:00 a.m. to 10:00 p.m., NO FEE

SHADES BEACH COUNTY PARK, Six miles east of Erie, CLASS A BOATS ONLY

NORTHEAST ACCESS AREA, Maintained by Fish Commission, two miles east of Junction of Rt. 5 and Rt. 89 at Dewey Road, NO FEE.

The public launching site at Walnut Creek, Lake Erie, an excellent facility maintained by the Fish Commission.

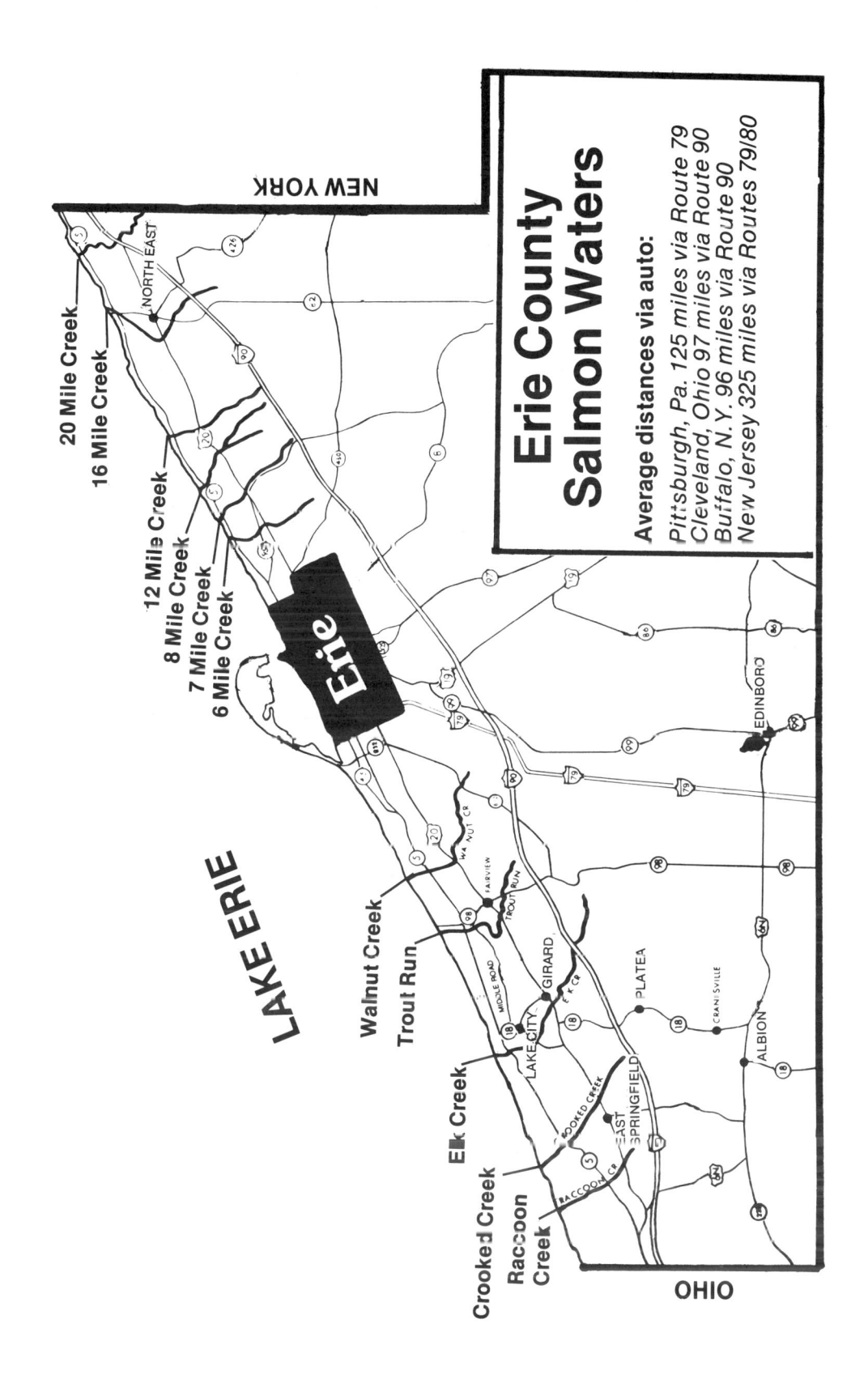

Erie County Salmon Waters

Average distances via auto:

Pittsburgh, Pa. 125 miles via Route 79
Cleveland, Ohio 97 miles via Route 90
Buffalo, N.Y. 96 miles via Route 90
New Jersey 325 miles via Routes 79/80

- 20 Mile Creek
- 16 Mile Creek
- 12 Mile Creek
- 8 Mile Creek
- 7 Mile Creek
- 6 Mile Creek
- Walnut Creek
- Trout Run
- Elk Creek
- Crooked Creek
- Raccoon Creek

STEELHEAD TROUT

The Steelhead trout is another large anadromous fish that returns to Erie County waters. Unlike the Coho and Chinooks that return in the fall, the Steelhead starts to make its appearance sometime in mid to late February. From that time forward they will be schooled just offshore and will periodically enter the tributary streams. They will continue to do so until about late May. About the early part of June they will retreat to the deeper cool waters of Lake Erie remaining from one to eight miles offshore. Properly equipped craft can locate and take them all during the hot weather using downriggers and spoons, and there are numerous launch sites available to the boat owner. (see our listing).

In early fall large number of Steelheads will appear in the streams, intermingled with the Coho and Chinooks. Persumably the Steelheads take advantage of the spawning runs of the Chinook and Coho to feast upon their freshly deposited eggs. During this time of year fishing is excellent from either the shoreline of the lake or from the banks of the streams.

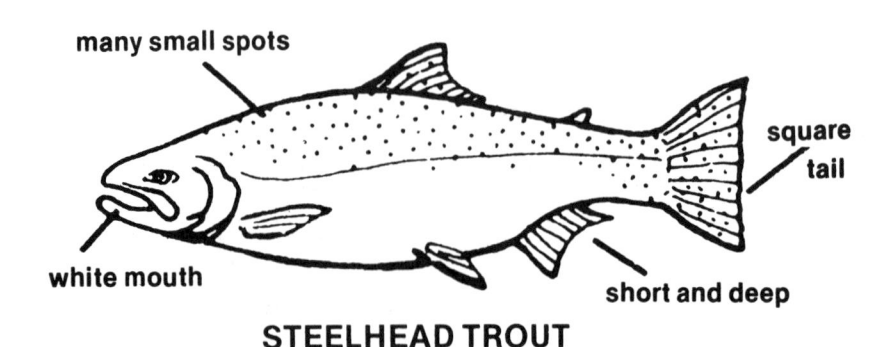

STEELHEAD TROUT

(spawning condition: reddish side stripe and somewhat enlarged jaw)

Becky Almy does a bit of fly fishing on a stretch of Spruce Creek, Huntingdon Co. This is a scenic stretch of water, plus fishing is excellent.

A day's catch of Coho Salmon, various sizes, all taken near the entrance of Walnut Creek.

The Steelheads will enter the same waters as detailed in the Coho/Chinook section of this guide, which are referenced on the Erie County map. There are some spawning areas that are OFF LIMITS to all angling and those areas when encountered will be clearly defined and must be avoided. The state record for Steelheads is 40¼ inches, 22 lb. 8 oz. However, their average size is closer to 30 inches and from 14 to 17 pounds. Sufficient tackle to handle these powerful fish is a must. Although most anglers will use spinning or bait casting equipment, they are a challenge to the flyrodder. If you wish to test your skill, use at least a 7-8 weight fly line, and an eight to ten pound test leader. Colorful streamers are your best bet, using at least a size six hook. Reds and golds work quite well.

During the past ten years various Erie County clubs have stocked well over 1,000,000 Steelheads into Lake Erie tributaries. Since they are not a spawn-and-perish fish like the salmon, it is safe to assume that several hundred thousand fish are thriving in the lake. Thousands are taken by the large number of anglers fishing during the warm weather. However, a great number are taken by the winter angler who are indeed a hardy and dedicated breed. Egg sacks from salmon or trout are the best winter baits. However, they can also be taken with streamers and assorted spoons and wobbling plugs.

Keep in mind that the daily limit is SIX COMBINED SPECIES of Coho, Chinook and Steelhead. There is no minimum size.

> In fly fishing you must match the weight of your rod, reel and line.

How to Choose a Fly Line if You Do Not Already Own a Fly Rod

1. **What kind of fish will you be fishing for?**

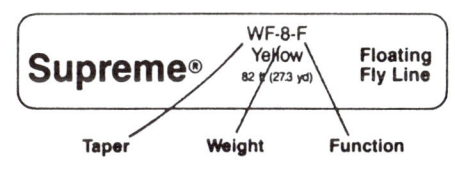

   Supreme® WF-8-F Yellow 82 g (27.3 yd) Floating Fly Line

   Taper — Weight — Function

   a. Trout/Panfish—recommended line weights 5, 6, or 7.6 weight is the best all around.
   b. Bass—recommended line weights 7, 8, or 9.7 weight is best all around.
   c. Salmon/Steelhead—recommended line weight 7, 8, 9, or 10.8 weight is the best all around.
   d. Saltwater—recommended line weights 9, 10, 11 or 12.10 weight is the best all around.

   Trout/Panfish—6 weight
   Bass/Salmon—8 weight

   The best compromise for all types of fishing is a 7 weight line.

2. **What type of fishing will you be doing?**
   a. Trout/Small Stream/Short Cast—A double taper (DT) line is recommended.
   b. Bass/Panfish/Salmon/Large Streams/Lakes/Long Cast—a weight forward (WF) line is recommended.

   The best compromise for all types of fishing is a weight forward (WF) line.

3. **Do you want a floating or sinking line?**
   a. Floating—Every fly fisherman should own a floating fly line.
   b. Sinking—To get flies down to the feeding level of the fish. Wet Cel II is a good all around choice.
   c. Floating/Sinking—Easier to use than full sinking lines. Wet Tip Hi-D is the best choice.

   The best compromise for most types of fishing is a Floating (F) fly line.

4. **What color fly line do you want?**
   a. White and light green (non-flourescent) are the most popular in floating lines.
   b. Flourescent colors are growing in popularity. Easy to see and control. They don't scare fish. Flourescent orange is the most popular.

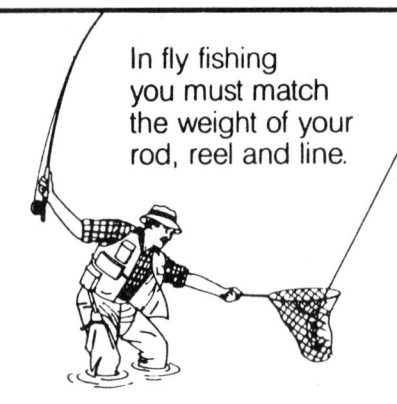

In fly fishing you must match the weight of your rod, reel and line.

How to Choose a Fly Line if You Already Own a Fly Rod

1. **What are the letters and numbers printed on the rod above the handle?**
   a. It should say something like **AFTMA 6** or **Line Weight 5/6** (either line weight wiil work) or sometimes just a number **8**, for example. Match the line weight specified on the rod to the line weight you buy. Line weights range from 3 (light) to 12 (heavy).

   LINE WT. NO. 8

   b. If you have an old rod with three letters (HDH, for example) printed on the rod or no numbers at all, the best way to determine the proper line weight is to try different lines on the rod. The following gives you a starting point if letters are provided.

2. **What type of fishing will you be doing?**
   a. Trout/Small Streams/ Short Cast—A double taper (DT) line is recommended.
   b. Bass/Panfish/Salmon/ Large Streams/Lakes/ Long Cast—a weight forward (WF) line is recommended.

   The best compromise for all types of fishing is a weight forward (WF) line.

3. **Do you want a floating or sinking line?**
   a. Floating—Every fly fisherman should own a floating fly line.
   b. Sinking—To get the flies down to the feeding level of the fish. Wet Cel II is a good all around choice.
   c. Floating/Sinking—Easier to use than full sinking lines. Wet Tip Hi-D is the best choice.

   The best compromise for most types of fishing is a Floating (F) fly line.

4. **What color fly line do you want?**
   Color is a matter of personal preference, however,
   a. White and light green (non-flourescent) are the most popular in floating lines.
   b. Flourescent colors are growing in popularity. Easy to see and control. They don't scare fish. Flourescent orange is the most popular.

Chart here correlates modern AFTMA line size numbers with traditional letter designations.

AFTMA No.	3	4	5	6	7	8	9	10	11	12
Double Taper (DT)	IGI	HFH	HEH	HDH	HCH	GBG	GAG	GAAG	G3AG	G4AG
Weight Forward (WF)	IGJ	HFG	HEG	HDG	HCF	GBF	GAF	GAAF	G3AF	G4AF
Shooting Taper (ST)	100 gr.	120 gr.	140 gr.	160 gr.	185 gr.	220 gr.	250 gr.	300 gr.	350 gr.	400 gr.

Utilizing The Insect Emergence Chart

In order to become a successful fly fisherman there is one aspect that should be examined; understanding and utilizng the emergence of insects that occurs in trout streams to match your lure. All trout, whether wild or hatchery reared, are dependent upon feeding cycles that are triggered during periods of emerging insect hatches. Even a recently stocked trout will adapt to the surroundings and can be observed rising for hatches as often as the day they are stocked.

In order to increase your overall skills as a fly fisherman, you should become familiar with the schedule of hatches that will occur on your favorite trout streams. More importantly, you must have in your fly box the exact imitation of the hatch in progress. It is important to know that trout, although frenzied feeders during periods of hatch activity, are quite selective, you must mach the emerging insect with an exact duplicate. If it is not similar to the real thing, chances are the trout will ignore it. When trout are feeding, they can be taken with relative ease provided you have the correct pattern. If not, it can be a long and painful time watching trout rise and resisting your presentation.

If you have some doubts as to the exact insect emerging, you should attempt to capture one of the live insects and compare it to those patterns in your box that bears close resemblance. If you cannot match the live hatch, you might take along the necessary fly tying tools and materials and tie one on the spot. Many fly fishermen are very adept at streamside fly tying and if you intend to become a dedicated fly fisherman, take the time and effort to be prepared for any unforeseen situation.

As a guide to charting the various hatches of trout streams, please refer to the enclosed EMERGENCE CHART, which will serve as a general guideline for the time of season you plan to be in the stream. Hatches are approximate and may vary according to weather and stream conditions.

(See page 16)

TROUT RECIPES

Now that you have successfully landed your trout, you will do one of two things; you will carefully disengage the hook and return the trout to the water, or you will determine if the fish meets the legal size requirement. If it does, it will go into your creel. For those anglers who fish not only for the joy of catching but also for the pleasure of consuming, eating can be as rewarding as catching, provided the trout has been properly prepared for the table. To give the reader a variety of preparation methods, we offer some delicious menus that are guaranteed to please your taste buds.

BAKED TROUT WITH LEMON — Dry the trout and salt both inside and out, then cover with seasoned flour. Place in a pan, and add one to two tablespoons of corn oil per trout. Before placing in the oven, cover each trout with a liberal amount of butter, adding some paprika. Bake at 375 degrees for about 20 minutes, 10 minutes per side. After baking, pour lemon sauce over the trout and place under the broiler until brown, browning one side only. Garnish with lemon wedges and parsley. (Lemon sauce is made by blending the juice of one lemon with a generous portion of butter or margarine.)

FOIL BAKED TROUT — Clean trout, removing head if desired. Place trout on a sheet of foil. Prepare a mix by melting one stick of margarine or butter, adding a packet of dry soup mix (onion). Cover the trout with a generous amount of mix, close foil and place on cookie sheet for baking. Bake at 350 degrees for 30 minutes.

TROUT AND BACON — Stuff the trout with half of lemon, adding butter. Wrap the trout with one or two strips of bacon, securing with toothpicks. Sprinkle with salt and pepper and broil each side for 10 minutes.

TROUT IN WHITE WINE — Season trout with salt and pepper. Place in buttered casserole and sprinkle juice of one lemon and ½ cup white wine over trout. Cover and bake in moderate over at 350 degrees for 15 minutes. Pour ½ cup of heavy cream over fish and place under broiler until sauce is brown. Keep broiler door open and watch carefully! Serve hot.